The Realist Short Story of the Powerful Glimpse

The Realist Short Story of the
Powerful Glimpse: Chekhov to Carver

Kerry McSweeney

THE UNIVERSITY OF SOUTH CAROLINA PRESS

© 2007 University of South Carolina

Published by the University of South Carolina Press
Columbia, South Carolina 29208

www.sc.edu/uscpress

Manufactured in the United States of America

16 15 14 13 12 11 10 09 08 07   10 9 8 7 6 5 4 3 2 1

Library of Congress Cataloging-in-Publication Data

McSweeney, Kerry, 1941–
  The realist short story of the powerful glimpse : Chekhov to Carver / Kerry McSweeney.
    p. cm.
  Includes bibliographical references and index.
  ISBN-13: 978-1-57003-695-8 (cloth : alk. paper)
  ISBN-10: 1-57003-695-0 (cloth : alk. paper)
  1. Realism in literature. 2. Literature, Modern—19th century—History and criticism.
  3. Literature, Modern—20th century—History and criticism. 4. Short story. I. Title.
  PN3340.M37 2007
  809.3'10912—dc22

                                                                    2006103021

For Susan and Ben

Contents

Preface

My subjects are the short stories of Anton Chekhov (1860–1904), James Joyce (1882–1941), Ernest Hemingway (1899–1961), Flannery O'Connor (1925–1964), and Raymond Carver (1939–1988). Why bring together writers from widely different generational, national, and cultural backgrounds? Not in order to study influence, although as we shall see, the web of connections among them has many strands. One reason is that they are all committed to the realist representation of experience and share a belief in the importance and efficacy of the short-story form. Clustering their work provides an opportunity to examine the strategies and assess the claims of realist short fiction. A second reason is that, as Richard L. Levin remarks, "no literary work . . . can ever be understood until it is placed in some prior and larger contexts. . . . The real problem . . . is not *whether* a literary work requires a context . . . but rather *which* contexts, or which kinds of contexts, should be chosen to understand *this* particular work" (1989, 89).

Carver located himself in a tradition of short-story writing that included O'Connor, Hemingway, Joyce, and, at its source, Chekhov—"the greatest short story writer who ever lived" because of "the awesome frequency with which he produced masterpieces, stories that shrive us as well as delight and move us" (*Call*, 219). In the various comments Carver made on short-story writing in essays and interviews, he had occasion to praise, quote, and paraphrase all these writers. When these comments are clustered, supplemented by comments of the other writers, and critically scrutinized, as they are in my introduction, the result is a thumbnail poetics of realist short fiction by some of the most distinguished practitioners of the form. I am hardly the first to have provided such a context. Charles E. May's "Chekhov and the Modern Short Story," for example, has expertly surveyed the same body of material from a literary-historical perspective. And others, such as Suzanne C. Ferguson in her "Defining the Short Story: Impressionism and Form," have offered generic overviews. The intent of my synoptic introduction is different: to develop an aesthetic critical model for more detailed considerations of the short stories of my subjects that brings distinctive features of the work of each into sharp focus, facilitates making qualitative discriminations among stories, and provides a basis for assessing the profitability of other critical models.

Each of the chapters on individual authors pursues one or more of the lines of inquiry opened in the introduction. The chapter on Chekhov distinguishes aesthetic readings of his stories from interpretative readings with particular reference to the recent spate of Christian exegetical attention his work has received. A number of Chekhov's finest stories are discussed, including "Anyuta," "In the Cart," "Gusev," "Ionych," "Easter Night," and "The Student." The subject of the second chapter is the first three stories in Joyce's *Dubliners*—"The Sisters," "An Encounter," and "Araby." I discuss the difference between essentialist and constructionist readings of these "stories of my childhood," as the author called them, with particular reference to the usefulness of cultural-studies models of critical discourse. The fourth chapter, on Hemingway's Nick Adams stories, picks up on an aspect of the previous chapter—the affective dynamics of interrelationship among stories in a sequence. This is one coordinate of a detailed consideration of three stories—"Indian Camp," "Big Two-Hearted River," and "Fathers and Sons." Other coordinates are Hemingway's comments on his method and genetic materials (drafts and deleted passages).

The fifth chapter is devoted to the Christian realism of Flannery O'Connor and considers the compatibility of the terms of that oxymoronic phrase. O'Connor's chosen form, the essential features of which she has well described, is the realist short story of Chekhov and Joyce as mediated by the American New Criticism. I argue that a number of her stories, including some of her finest, do not depend on the operation of supernatural grace and that in other stories divine causation remains bracingly problematic. The next chapter assesses Carver's achievement as a short-story writer, beginning with his early re-inscription of Hemingway's "Big Two-Hearted River" and ending with a consideration of his last story, "Errand," the subject of which is the death of his literary master, Chekhov. The final chapter suggests the advantages of the model used in this study for reading other realist short stories.

As a relative newcomer to thinking about the short story as a literary form, I much profited from works such as Susan Lohafer and Jo Ellyn Clarey's *Short Story Theory at a Crossroads* (1989) and Charles E. May's *The New Short Story Theories* (1994). But as will be seen, my principal methodological and theoretical reference points derive from my major professional interests over the past three decades—the realist novel and the poetry of the nineteenth century. In my work on the latter I became interested in developing an aesthetic critical model as an alternative to theory-driven interpretative models. In time, I came to feel that a similar model could be equally useful for the study of my subjects' short stories, many of which (as has long been recognized) are more lyric than plot-driven and more spatial than linear, and to realize that such a model could be extrapolated from their own critical comments. Over this period, I received advice and encouragement from numerous persons. My gratitude to most of them has been acknowledged in other places. Here I would like particularly to thank Lyudmila Parts of the McGill University Department of Russian, who mediated my engagement with Chekhov's stories; the anonymous reader for *Modern Language Studies,* in which an earlier version of the second half of my Chekhov chapter first appeared; Barry Blose; my McGill colleagues Allan Hepburn, Peter Sabor, and David Williams; and, as always, my wife, Susanne.

Note on Texts and Citations

Unless otherwise noted, the text for all quotations from Carver's stories is *Where I'm Calling From: New and Selected Stories.* The following abbreviations are used in citations from Carver's essays and from interviews with him: *Call* for *Call Me If You Need Me* and *Conv* for *Conversations with Raymond Carver,* ed. Gentry and Stull.

Wherever possible, the text for quotations from Chekhov's stories is *Stories,* trans. Richard Pevear and Larissa Volokhonsky. The text for quotations from *The Steppe* and *Three Years* is the same translators' *The Complete Short Novels.* For other stories, the following translations have been used:

"Enemies" from *A Doctor's Visit and Other Stories,* ed. Tobias Wolff

"In the Cart" and "About Love" from *About Love and Other Stories,* trans. Rosamund Bartlett

"Ionych" from *Lady with Lapdog and Other Stories,* trans. David Margarshack

"A Nervous Breakdown" from *The Party and Other Stories,* trans. Ronald Wilks

"Agafya" and "Peasants" from *Selected Stories,* trans. Ann Dunnigan

Unless otherwise noted, the text for all quotations from Hemingway's stories is *The Short Stories of Ernest Hemingway* (Scribner's Modern Standard Authors).

The text for all quotations from *Dubliners* is the Oxford World's Classics edition, ed. Jeri Johnson.

The text for all quotations from O'Connor's stories is *The Complete Stories*. The following abbreviations are used in citations from her letters and essays: *HB* for *The Habit of Being: Letters* and *MM* for *Mystery and Manners: Occasional Prose*.

Introduction

1

Good writers, Raymond Carver observes, are different from each other in that each possesses a distinctive sensibility that puts "a particular and unmistakable signature on everything he writes." They have "some special way of looking at things and [give] artistic expression to that way of looking" (*Call*, 87–88). The writers Carver most admires are those "concerned with writing accurately, that is to say, thoughtfully and carefully, about recognizable men and women and children going about the sometimes ordinary business of living . . . who find themselves in more or less critical situations" (*Call*, 214; *Conv*, 184). But within this spectrum of realist representation there are a variety of presentational vehicles—of ways "of looking at things." Carver was himself "drawn toward the traditional (some would call it old-fashioned) methods of storytelling: one layer of reality unfolding and giving way to another, perhaps richer layer; the gradual accretion of meaningful detail; dialogue that not only reveals something about character but advances the story" (*Call*, 210).

While this may sound traditional, Carver's own stories have little in common with the work of many accomplished nineteenth- and twentieth-century practitioners of the short story. The narrator of W. Somerset Maugham's "The Human Element," for example, clearly speaks for the author when he says that he likes "a story to have a beginning, a middle, and an end. I have a weakness for a point." And *in proprio persona* Maugham distinguishes the Maupassant line in twentieth-century short stories from the Chekhov line in a way that displays a clear preference for the former. The French writer's stories "are good stories. The anecdote is interesting apart from the narration so that it would secure attention if it were told over the dinner-table; and that seems to me a very great merit indeed. . . . These stories . . . do not wander along an uncertain line, so that you cannot see whither they are leading, but follow without hesitation, from exposition to climax, a bold and vigorous curve" (1967, 2:995; 1963, 46).[1]

It is to this kind of story that Carver is referring when he admits that "I greatly admire stories that unfold in that classic mode, with conflict, resolution, and denouement. But even though I can respect those stories, and sometimes even be a little envious, I can't write them" (*Conv,* 111). Nor could Joyce or Chekhov. Ezra Pound explained in his review of *Dubliners* in the *Egoist* in 1914 that Joyce "is not bound by the tiresome convention that any part of life, to be interesting, must be shaped into the conventional form of a 'story.' Since De Maupassant we have had so many people trying to write 'stories' and so few people presenting life. Life for the most part does not happen in neat little diagrams and nothing is more tiresome than the continual pretence that it does" (1954, 400). As for Chekhov, it was his innovation to write stories that were not heavily plotted and omitted traditional exposition, development, and closure. Inter alia, this led the early-twentieth-century readers for whom Virginia Woolf is speaking in the following passage to ask of the close of a Chekhov story: "But is it the end? we ask. We rather have the feeling that we have overrun our signals; or it is as if a tune had stopped short without the expected chords to close it. These stories are inconclusive, we say, and proceed to frame a criticism based upon the assumption that stories ought to conclude in a way that we recognize" (1966, 1:240).

Chekhov's and Carver's short stories have more in common with lyric poems than with novels "in what the writing is aiming for, in the compression of language and emotion, and in the care and control required to achieve their effects. . . . You're trying to capture and hold a moment. A

---

1. A similar distinction is made by Henry James, but this writer and critic valorizes the kind of story Maugham demotes. In a review written in 1898, James asks:

> Are there not two quite distinct effects to be produced by the rigor of brevity . . . ? The one with which we are most familiar is that of the detached incident, single and sharp, as clear as a pistol-shot; the other, of rarer performance, is that of the impression, comparatively generalised—simplified, foreshortened, reduced to a particular perspective—of a complexity or a continuity. The former is an adventure comparatively safe, in which you have, for the most part, but to put one foot after the other. It is just the risks of the latter, on the contrary, that make the best of the sport. These are naturally—given the general reduced scale—immense, for nothing is less intelligible than bad foreshortening, which, if it fails to mean everything intended, means less than nothing. (1984, 1:285)

novel is an accretion of detail that may cover weeks or months or years. . . . The story takes place in a much smaller compass of time, just like the poem" (*Conv*, 105–6; 187). Citing V. S. Pritchett's pictorial figuration of the short story as "something glimpsed from the corner of the eye, in passing," Carver describes the writer's task as being to "invest the glimpse with all that is in his power. . . . First the glimpse. Then the glimpse given life, turned into something that will illuminate the moment and just maybe lock it indelibly into the reader's consciousness" (*Call*, 92, 201). But Carver could just as well have cited his master, Chekhov, who observed that it is "compactness that makes short things live. . . . Long, detailed works have their own peculiar aims, which require a most careful execution regardless of the total impression. But in short stories it is better not to say enough than to say too much, because,—because—I don't know why!" (1965, 82, 106).

A good example of the Chekhovian glimpse is "The Huntsman," a story with an intertextual dimension that alludes to, as it swerves from, the Turgenevian gaze of "The Meeting" (or "The Tryst") from *Sketches from a Hunter's Album* (see Bitsilli 1983, 15–16). Both one-scene stories describe a country meeting between two peasants—a hopelessly-in-love female and an indifferent male who has become socially superior to her. The precursor story is about 4,000 words long and devotes 1,300 of them to detailed description of the natural setting and the weather, and of the lovely Akulina and the preening and overdressed Victor Alexandrych. Chekhov's re-inscription is less than 2,000 words long, dispensing with both visual specification and the framing device of an educated and sensitive first-person narrator who observes the meeting and is moved by the pathos of the woman's plight. In Chekhov's story, there is as much social context as in Turgenev's—but it is intimated in a few strokes. The title character, Yegor Vlasych, is a huntsman on the staff of a rural estate who has become used to a comparatively easy life, despite his master's demeaning treatment of him. His legal wife, Pelageya, with whom he has never lived, is an agricultural laborer—"a pale-faced woman of about thirty with a sickle in her hand" (a dozen words of description as opposed the nearly 400 Turgenev devotes to Akulina). The setting, sketched in the story's opening lines, evokes Pelageya's condition of being: "A sultry and stifling day. Not a cloud in the sky. . . . The sun-scorched grass looks bleak, hopeless: there may be rain, but it will never be green again. . . . The forest stands silent, motionless, as if its treetops were looking off somewhere or waiting for something" (ellipses in original). A chance encounter with her husband brings an unsuppressible joy to Pelageya—she gazes on him tenderly, "laughs like a fool. . . . Her own face breathes happiness . . . ashamed of her joy, [she] covers her smiling mouth with her hand." When three ducks fly over, Yegor follows them with his eyes until they become specks. In saying goodbye, he gives her a worn rouble and then walks away with his hunting dog. She follows him with her eyes and—in the story's closing words—"stands on tiptoe so as at least to see the white cap one more time." The story is over as quickly as the "soft song" from the harvested rows "which breaks off at the very beginning. It is too hot for singing" (9–12). But the pathos of Pelageya's situation has been affectingly communicated. The reader, so to speak, stands on tiptoe with her at the end of the story and needs no surrogate within the text to show him or her how to be moved.

But it must not be forgotten that "glimpse" is a figurative, not a literal, term and is used by Carver suggestively, not prescriptively. While numbers of Chekhov's stories, and many of Hemingway's and his own, take place in "real time" or an approximation of it and observe the unities of place and action, such concision is not the defining feature of their short stories. One of Chekhov's greatest stories, "The Lady with the Little Dog," for example, takes place over the period of a year and is successively set in Yalta, a unnamed provincial city, and Moscow. In visual terms, it is not the temporal and spatial limits of observation but rather intensity of focus that is the prerequisite for a powerful impression.

2

For Carver, another sine qua non of a powerful impression is "clear and specific language, language used so as to bring to life the details that will light up the story for the reader. For the details to be concrete and convey meaning, the language must be accurate and precisely given" (*Call*, 92). In his own fiction, Carver tries to "eliminate every single unnecessary detail [and] to cut my words to the bone" (*Conv*, 80). He believes "in the efficacy of the concrete word, be it noun or verb, as opposed to the abstract or arbitrary or slippery word—or phrase, or sentence"; "if the words are in any way blurred the reader's eyes will slide right over them and nothing will be achieved. The reader's own artistic sense will simply not be engaged" (*Call*, 211, 90). Carver deplores "sloppy or haphazard writing whether it flies under the banner of experimentation or else is just clumsily rendered realism. In Isaac Babel's wonderful short story 'Guy de Maupassant' the narrator has this to say about the writing of fiction: 'No iron can stab the heart with such force as a period put just at the right place.' This too ought to go on a three-by-five"—the reference is to the index cards Carver taped to the wall beside his writing desk (*Call*, 89–90).

Hemingway is another admirer of Babel's style, which he is said to have described as "even more concise than mine, which is more wordy. It shows what can be done. Even when you've got all the water out of them, you can still clot the curds a bit more" (Ehrenburg 1969, 236). And in numerous letters, Chekhov chastises other writers for their prolixity. But there is more than one mode of clear and concise writing, and it would be misleading to give the impression that the prose styles of my five subjects are essentially similar. To cite the sentence in Babel's "Guy de Maupassant" that comes immediately before the one Carver quoted: style can be thought of as "an army of words, an army in which every type of weapon is deployed." These weapons include Chekhov's literary impressionism; the "scrupulous meanness" of the *Dubliners* stories, which bespeaks Joyce's "conviction that he is a very bold man who dares to alter in the presentment, still more to deform, whatever he has seen and heard" (1975, 83); Hemingway's reportorial terseness; Flannery O'Connor's extensive use of similes and *as if* constructions; and what has been described as Carver's "privation of image and metaphor [that] lays an air of desolation thickly around his stories" (Arias-Misson 1982, 626).

It should also be noted that within the corpus of each writer's short fiction, and even within individual stories, there are different stylistic registers. Hemingway, for example, sometimes writes in a style less reportorial than Imagist, bringing "language to the intensity of image through ironic use of context and through presentation in repetitive patterns" (Benson 1990, 285). An example is the metonymically rich opening paragraph of "In Another Country": "In the fall the war was always there, but we did not go to it any more. It was cold in the fall in Milan and the dark came very early. Then the electric lights came on, and it was pleasant along the streets looking in the windows. There was much game hanging outside the shops, and the snow powdered in the fur of the foxes and the wind blew their tails. The deer hung stiff and heavy and empty, and small birds blew in the wind and the wind turned their feathers. It was a cold fall and the wind came down from the mountains" (267). Here the cadenced parataxis, verbal and syntactic repetition, and precise details give the sense less of something being seen than of someone intensely—even obsessively—seeing. In this context, as David Lodge has noted, details of "the game hanging outside the shops inevitably function as symbols of death and destruction" (1977, 159).

As for Joyce's stories: while always scrupulous, the style is not always mean in the sense of laconic notation of low particulars such as "the cabbage [that] began to deposit a cold white grease" on Mr. Duffy's plate in

"A Painful Case" and the workingmen in the same story who drank and smoked, "spitting often on the floor and sometimes dragging the sawdust over their spits with their heavy boots." In *Dubliners*, Joyce also appropriates, mimes, and/or parodies literary and spoken discourses, and the voice of his narrators sometimes blends with the thoughts of the stories' protagonists in ways that produce a variety of effects. Examples are the Celtic Twilight impressionism of Little Chandler's response to a cityscape in "A Little Cloud" and Gabriel Conroy's vision at the end of "The Dead" of "the snow falling faintly through the universe and faintly falling" (86, 89, 176). It is this linguistic versatility and fluency and not simply the scrupulous meanness per se that comprise Joyce's distinctive stylistic signature in *Dubliners*.

3

Another essential feature of a realist short story is what Carver calls "meaningful detail" (*Conv*, 198). It is possible, he insists, "to write about commonplace things and objects using commonplace but precise language, and to endow those things—a chair, a window curtain, a fork, a stone, a woman's earring—with immense, even startling power" (*Call*, 89). Certainly it goes without saying that in the restricted space of a short story, as compared with a novel, there is or should be a much higher proportion of functional details. This is especially true of stories in the manner of Chekhov that express inner states of character by means of selected concrete details. One needs to distinguish among these functions even while recognizing that they are not mutually exclusive and that a single detail can perform more than one task.

One function is to contribute to the true-to-life feel of the story; another is to vivify and intensify the impression. To serve these ends, details in short fiction should be sparingly deployed. Too many details, as Chekhov observed, lead to "an overwrought 'motleyness' of effect that impairs the general impression" (1965, 106). One or a few items make for crispness; extensive particularization leads to sogginess. An example of the former is this description of Ignatius Gallaher in Joyce's "A Little Cloud": "[He] took off his hat and displayed a large closely cropped head. His face was heavy, pale and clean-shaven. His eyes, which were of bluish slate-colour, relieved his unhealthy pallor and shone out plainly above the vivid orange tie he wore. Between these rival features the lips appeared very long and shapeless and colourless. He bent his head and felt with two sympathetic fingers the thin hair at the crown" (56). I cannot understand Sean O'Faolain's complaints about the lack of compression in this passage and about words he finds "not always well-chosen": "Is it true that Ignatius Gallaher 'displayed' his head? That word implies that he wished to show his baldness . . . 'Rival features.' Is a tie a feature?" (1964, 225). It is indeed the case that Gallaher, a compulsive showoff, is displaying his thinning hair to his meek inter-locutor. And the tie is an integral feature of this cameo description: the clash of bluish slate and vivid orange nicely intimates the abrasive tastelessness of Gallaher's personality.

The many examples in Chekhov's fiction of a striking single notation include phrases I have italicized in the following sentences: "Nikolai Chik-ildeyev, a waiter in the Slavyansky Bazaar, a hotel in Moscow, had fallen ill. His legs went numb and his walk was affected, so that one day, as he was going along the corridor *carrying a trayful of ham and peas,* he stumbled and fell" ("Peasants," 242); at a meal after the funeral of her infant, "Lipa served at the table, and the priest, *raising a fork with a pickled mushroom on it,* said to her: 'Don't grieve over the baby. Of such is the Kingdom of Heaven'" ("In the Ravine," 415). These examples also illustrate another function of detail: to be telling—to metonymically exemplify, to have characterologi-cal, social, or thematic suggestiveness. In their immediate contexts, both details vivify; but they are also telling in the larger context of the stories that contain them—the two Chekhov stories most explicitly critical of the social and economic conditions in Russia. The fare served at the Moscow hotel is very different from the sustenance available in the impoverished peasant hut in his native village, to which the dying Chikildeyev and his family must return after he loses his job. And the notation of clerical inges-tion at the funeral meal in "In the Ravine" recalls the opening notation in the story's depiction of the physical and moral squalor of the industrial vil-lage of Ukleyevo: the only thing people ever remembered about the place was that at a memorial dinner another cleric once consumed four pounds of caviar without stopping.

As for descriptions of nature, Chekhov told another writer: "In such sto-ries as yours, descriptions of Nature are in place and do not detract from the effect only when they are à propos, when they help you communicate to the reader this or that mood." He further advised that a writer "ought to seize upon the little particulars, grouping them in such a way that, in read-ing, when you shut your eyes, you get a picture. For instance, you will get the full effect of a moonlight night if you write that on the mill-dam a lit-tle glowing star-point flashed from the neck of a broken bottle . . ." (1965, 74, 70–71). In his own natural descriptions, however, Chekhov was fre-quently able to be less terse and less exclusively visual without collapsing into a motley of weak specification because of the acuity and crispness of his notations—as in this description by the narrator of "Agafya" of the synesthetic enchantment of the coming of night in the kitchen garden of a rural village: "the darkness was growing thicker, and objects began to lose their contours. The strip of sky behind the hill had completely disappeared and the stars grew brighter and more luminous. The mournful, monotonous chirping of the grasshoppers, the corncrake's cry, the calling of the quails, did not destroy the night's tranquillity but, on the contrary, only served to swell the great monotone. The soft sounds, enchanting to the ear, seemed not to come from birds and insects, but from the stars looking down upon us from the sky" (87).

In reading Chekhov's stories, one must learn to distinguish between the objective natural descriptions of the narrator and the subjective impressions of a particular character. The latter are frequently revealing of the character's psychological state. But as ever in a short story, the effect depends upon the crispness of the notation and the implicitness of the communication. An early Chekhov story provides an striking example of how not to do it when it comes to communicating mood through natural description. In "Enemies," two men, each in a state of acute psychological distress, are traveling together at night along a road: "In all nature one felt something hopeless and sick. Like a fallen woman who sits alone in a dark room trying not to think of her past, the earth languished with reminiscence of spring and summer and waited in apathy for ineluctable winter. Wherever one's glance turned, nature showed everywhere like a dark, cold, bottomless pit" (11).

A successful example is found in Chekhov's last story, "The Fiancée." When Nadya looks out her bedroom window at dawn, she sees "the densely flowering lilac bushes, sleepy and languid from the cold; and dense white mist is slowly drifting towards the lilacs, wanting to cover them." This registers her nocturnal anxieties about her approaching marriage. But later, when the sun is up and the mist has left the garden, it is Nadya's youthfulness and vibrant spirits that are suggested: "Soon the whole garden revived, warmed and caressed by the sun, and dewdrops sparkled like diamonds on the leaves" (441). It might be argued that in such descriptions natural details should be considered symbols; but in reading Chekhov's stories, it is insensitive not to distinguish this intimacy of interconnection between perceiver and perceived from the conceptual transference involved in symbolic readings. The former is frequently signaled by the verb *seem* or the phrase "for some reason." The absence of either marker in the description of what Nadya sees from her bedroom window makes for an intensified effect—in figurative terms the description is an example of hypallage or transferred epithet.

Still other details are meaningful in the sense that they have conceptual implications—that is, they are symbolic objects. As Flannery O'Connor explains: "The short story requires more drastic procedures than the novel because more has to be accomplished in less space. The details have to carry more immediate weight. In good fiction, certain of the details will tend to accumulate meaning from the story itself, and when this happens, they become symbolic in their action" (*MM*, 70). But how is one to determine when a concrete detail should be taken to stand for something abstract? The answer is that a great deal of critical tact is required of readers, who must make crucial determinations concerning when to read symbolically and when not to. Consider, for example, a detail from Chekhov's "The Lady with the Little Dog." It is found in the hotel room Gurov has rented in the provincial city he has come to in order to see Anna again: "there was an inkstand on the table, gray with dust, with a horseback rider, who held his hat in his raised hand, but whose head was broken off" (370). This item has been called "symbolic" by one commentator, though of what he does not say (Debreczeny 2002, xx), while another opines: "If we recall how Gurov had raged at his wasted past life then it is easy to recognize that the horseman is Gurov himself, mindlessly (headlessly) galloping through life, forever bowing (= raising his hat) to the conventional philistine values of his society" (Rosen 1985, 20). In contrast, I would be content to regard the inkstand as a vivid detail that is telling in the sense of exemplifying *poshlost*—the inferior taste and repellent mediocrity of provincial life. To give it a symbolic meaning cited above is to turn the inkstand into a crude moralizing device that is surely antithetical to the subtlety and suggestiveness of Chekhov's great love story.

Before one decides to read a detail in a realist short story symbolically, I suggest several caveats. One is not to use the term *symbol* before considering whether another term is not more appropriate: for example, *image* ("Characterized by [its] evocation of *concrete qualities* rather than abstract meanings" [Hawthorn 2001, 109]) or *motif* ("a minimal thematic unit" [Prince 1987, 55]; "a discrete thing, image, or phrase that is repeated in a narrative" [Abbott 2002, 193]). Another is to distinguish between metonymy/synecdoche (contiguity or part for whole) and metaphor (similarity, resemblance) and not call an object a symbol unless there is both a metonymic and a metaphorical aspect to the relationship of signifier to signified. Another important distinction is between objects that have a symbolic meaning for characters and objects whose symbolic dimensions can be assigned to the implied author. The former is an aspect of characterization. In Carver's "Gazebo," for example, the title object refers to something a wife remembers during a day she and her husband spend in drunken argument over his mindless adultery. Her memory is of a day in the country when they had stopped at a farmhouse to ask for a glass of water and noticed a gazebo in the back. "I thought we'd like that too when we got old enough," she reflects. "Dignified. And in a place. And people would come to our door" (146). In an ungenerous assessment of Carver's stories in his *Talents and Technicians: Literary Chic and the New Assembly–Line Fiction,* John W. Aldridge claims that "Carver obviously intended this pastoral recollection to suggest what it is that the couple may have lost with the disintegration of their love and marriage. But it is actually specious, sentimental, and dramatically unearned" (1992, 54). But what should be obvious is that it is the wife, not the author, for whom the gazebo has symbolic value. As such, it perfectly captures an aspect of the life of the working poor—the moment when, in Studs Terkel's formulation, "the hard substance of the daily job fuses to the haze of the daydream" (1974, xx).

A final caveat is that the function of a detail can change over the course of a story—for example, the snow in Chekhov's "A Nervous Breakdown." When initially described, the first winter snowfall seems a natural correlative of the high spirits of three young men who are singing as they walk through Moscow on their way to the street of brothels: "The air smelt of snow; snow softly crunched underfoot; the ground, roofs, trees, boulevard benches—all was soft, white and new, and the houses looked quite different from the day before. The lamps shone more brightly, the air was clearer and the clatter of carriages was muffled. And one's sensations became just like the touch of white, new, fluffy snow, in that fresh, light frosty air." When next described, the snow is seen from the subjective viewpoint of the most sensitive and innocent of the three, the law student Vasilyev, who is paying his first visit to what he thinks of as fallen women: "He liked the snow. . . . He liked the air and particularly that crystal-clear, gentle, innocent, almost virginal mood that one sees in nature only twice a year." But Vasilyev is profoundly shocked, indeed destabilized to the point of breakdown, by the discovery of what brothels and their prostitutes are actually like. The final description of the snow occurs later as he waits in the street: "If one looked up at this darkness, the entire black background was sprinkled with moving white dots—falling snow. When the flakes came into the light they circled lazily in the air, like down, then fell even more lazily to earth. A mass of them swirled around Vasilyev and clung to his beard, eyelashes, eyebrows" (211, 212, 223). Here the point of view is that of the narrator, not the student, and the black background and lazily falling snow sticking to the young man's face suggest the effect of his experience on his inner being.

The standard definition of a literary symbol is something concrete that through conceptual transference is made to stand for or suggest something abstract. But an effective symbol in realist short fiction is seldom so cut-and-dried as this. Many symbols carry affective as well as conceptual implications; their significance and power are not dependent merely on the cognitive act of decoding but rather on a fully engaged and integrated reading. They are not emphatic and explicit, but deeply embedded and implicit. As one critic has put it, these details belong "equally to two realms —the 'real' and the symbolic. [They do] not burn with an even glow, but flicker, first with a symbolic glow and then with a 'real' light" (Chudakov 1983, 131). Or, to use an auditory rather than a visual image, they *ping*.

When a *ping* is too loud, it becomes a *thud* and can have a negative impact on one's reception of a realist short story. In one of Carver's, for example, the noise begins with the title, "The Bridle." This object is found by the landlady in the accommodation just vacated by the shiftless Holits family. It had value for Mr. Holits as a token of his passion for horses and betting on them. But in the story's last paragraph it is showcased as an authorial symbol for what the punishing force of quotidian struggle is doing to him and his family: "That part's called the bit. It's made of steel. Reins go over the head and up to where they're held on the neck between the fingers. The rider pulls the reins this way and that, and the horse turns. It's simple. The bit's heavy and cold. If you had to wear this thing between your teeth, I guess you'd catch on in a hurry. When you felt it pull, you'd know it was time. You'd know you were going somewhere" (*Cathedral,* 208). Not only is this overt and insistent; it is also indecorous in that the voice of the first-person narrator—the poorly spoken landlady—is overwritten by the more articulate and evocative voice of the implied author. Carver has said that he prefers "as with Chekhov's stories . . . the light touch in this matter of how consequence is delivered" (*Call,* 229). But in this case, his touch is heavy.

This is not to imply that there is no place for flagrant signifiers in realist short stories. It is a question of the fictional contract. Flannery O'Connor's mode of realist representation, for example, can accommodate emphatic effects that Joyce's or Hemingway's modes cannot. Consider her story "Good Country People," in which a female doctor of philosophy, living with her mother in the country, has her wooden leg stolen by a Bible salesman she is trying to seduce in a hayloft. The author herself has provided a fine explication of the story's central detail—the wooden leg:

Early in the story, we're presented with the fact that the Ph.D. is spiritually as well as physically crippled. She believes in nothing but her own belief in nothing, and we perceive that there is a wooden part of her soul that corresponds to her wooden leg. Now of course this is never stated. The fiction writer states as little as possible. The reader makes this connection from things he is shown. He may not even know that he makes the connection, but the connection is there nevertheless and it has an effect on him. As the story goes on, the wooden leg continues to accumulate meaning . . . and finally, by the time the Bible salesman comes along, the leg has accumulated so much meaning that it is, as the saying goes, loaded. And when the Bible salesman steals it, the reader realizes that he has taken away part of the girl's personality and has revealed her deeper affliction to her for the first time.

If you want to say that the wooden leg is a symbol, you can say that. But it is a wooden leg first, and as a wooden leg it is absolutely necessary to the story. It has its place on the literal level of the story, but it operates in depth as well as on the surface. It increases the story in every direction, and this is essentially the way a story escapes being short. (*MM,* 99–100)

But whether discrete or flaunted, all of the signifying objects I have been describing are similar in that they operate on a horizontal, not a vertical, axis. They do not signify entities or abstractions above and beyond the narratives that contain them. They are rather part of the represented world and accumulate meaning from the encompassing narrative.

4

In addition to compression, precision of language, and significant detail, Carver also emphasizes the importance of "the things that are left out, that are implied, the landscape under the smooth (but sometimes broken and unsettled) surface of things." This "goes back to Hemingway of course" (*Call,* 92; *Conv,* 126). The younger writer is referring to his predecessor's famous iceberg theory, the best-known formulation of which occurs in *Death in the Afternoon:* "If a writer of prose knows enough about what he is writing about he may omit things that he knows and the reader, if the writer is writing truly enough, will have a feeling of those things as strongly as though the writer had stated them. The dignity of movement of an ice-berg is due to only one-eighth of it being above water" (1932, 192).

This dictum has become so well known and so influential that one is initially taken aback by the cold eye cast on it by Flannery O'Connor: "many people decide that they want to write short stories because they're short, and by short, they mean short in every way. They think that a short story is an incomplete action in which a very little is shown and a great deal suggested, and they think you suggest something by leaving it out. It's very hard to disabuse a student of this notion, because he thinks that when he leaves something out, he's being subtle; and when you tell him he has to put something in before anything can be there, he thinks you're an insensitive idiot" (*MM*, 93–94). What are we really talking about when we talk about leaving things out and the effect of doing so? Is it something more than V. S. Pritchett's observation that because it is by definition succinct, a short story has "to suggest things that have been 'left out,' are, in fact, there all the time" (1981, xiv)? Are conscious omissions "designed to make audiences feel more than they understand" (Hallett 1996, 489)? Or is it the case that, as Clare Hanson argues, the restricted frame of the short story is a "formal property [that] permits ellipses (gaps and absences) to remain in a story, which retains a necessary air of completeness and order because of the very existence of the frame. We thus accept a degree of mystery, elision, uncertainty in the short story as we would not in the novel" (1989, 25)? As Carver insists, a story needs to contain "a sense of mystery, of something happening just under the surface of things. . . . There has to be tension, a sense that something is imminent, that certain things are in relentless motion, or else, most often, there simply won't be a story" (*Conv*, 198; *Call*, 92).

It is well to remember that the practice of leaving things out hardly began with Hemingway. For Chekhov, for example, this was a natural result of his compositional method: "I can only write from reminiscences, and I have never written direct from Nature. I have let my memory sift the subject, so that only what is important or typical is left in it as in a filter" (1965, 32). It was also the result of his insistence on objectivity: the compactness of a short story meant that "subjectivity"—that is, descriptions of the central character's state of mind—should be excluded: "When I write," Chekhov explains, "I reckon entirely upon the reader to add for himself the subjective elements that are lacking in the story. . . . In the sphere of psychology, details are . . . the thing. God preserve us from commonplaces. Best of all is to avoid depicting the hero's state of mind; you ought to try to make it clear from the hero's actions. . . . A writer must be as objective as a chemist: he must abandon the subjective line" (1965, 65, 71, 275).[2]

2. Other examples are found in the stories of Joyce's *Dubliners*. Harold F. Mosher Jr. has investigated "nonnarrated" features "like not naming or delaying the names of characters or objects, eliding words in dialogue, referring to but not reporting

One should also note that for Hemingway and Carver the technique of leaving things out is part of a larger strategy for transferring experience to the reader. "The best fiction," Carver insists, "should make such an impression that the work, as Hemingway suggested, becomes a part of the reader's experience" (*Call*, 223). The elder writer repeatedly emphasized the importance of this in his work. For example, he told George Plimpton that "I have tried to eliminate everything unnecessary to conveying experience to the reader so that after he or she has read something it will become a part of his or her experience and seem actually to have happened. This is very hard to do and I have worked at it very hard" (Plimpton 1963, 236). But Hemingway is here identifying only one of the devices he used for intensifying the reader's engagement with a story. As he remarked in a letter of 1933: "I am trying, always, to convey to the reader a full and complete feeling of the thing I am dealing with; to make the person reading feel it has happened to them [*sic*]. In doing this I have to use many expedients . . ." (1981, 380). One expedient, as Earl Rovit has explained, is to present sensations and perceptions "within a framework of physical or psychological stress, in which the narrative perspective is left open-ended so that the attentive reader is forced to serve as the 'ground' for the powerful prose-currents of the presented action" (1963, 25). Another, as Hemingway himself described it, is "mak[ing] the story . . . become a part of the reader's experience and his memory" by inserting "things that he did not notice when he read the story . . . which without his knowing it, enter into his memory and experience so that they are a part of his life" (1999, 5–6). These tactics are not the same as leaving things out and are arguably more important in making the reader feel that what is represented has happened to him or her.

5

It follows from Carver's valorization of traditional narrative methods and the representation of ordinary life that he is not interested "in haphazard revelations, attenuated characters, stories where method or technique is all." He does not like stories that "turn away from the concerns and techniques of realism"—such as those "short fictions à la Barthelme" that show

---

words characters must have said, not identifying antecedents for pronouns, leaving referents vague in characters' thoughts and speech, suppressing the thoughts of characters whose characters are otherwise revealed" (1993, 407). He argues that these make up a strategy of implication that both contributes to the story's brevity and helps create an illusion of expansion.

"a serious lack of interest and concern on the part of the author for his characters." In such works, the realist "pact or compact between the writer and the reader" is broken; "characters are set up and then they're set down again in some sort of subtle pratfall or awakening." Furthermore, "fiction about fiction or about the experience of writing fiction is not very viable or lasting. . . . I don't like to read about the experience of writing, the self-reflexive thing of writing fiction about writing fiction and so forth" (*Call*, 210, 239; *Conv*, 184–5, 210).

One can readily understand this animus in a writer who locates himself in the tradition of Chekhov. But just as there are self-conscious poems, so there are self-conscious stories—stories about a writer trying to write a story; stories with a reflexive subtext; stories with intertextual relationships to stories by other writers; stories containing embedded stories that, as John Barth remarks, "always to some degree imply stories *about* stories and even stories about story*telling*" (1984, 221); and stories that in other ways call attention to the medium of representation and foreground their status as a verbal construct. But does it follow that all such works are not fiction of occurrence and consequence, as Carver intimates? One might better distinguish between stories in which such features enrich the referential contract and deepen the reader's engagement in the story from those that break the contract and reduce the reading experience to a game.

Chekhov's "The Student," for example, is a story about the reception of another story and implicitly invites readers to become self-consciously aware of their reception of Chekhov's text. Carver's own story, "Put Yourself in My Shoes," is about a blocked writer's finding a subject (the story one is reading) in a social evening during which an obnoxious host repeatedly insists on describing real-life anecdotes of the tabloid kind and urging the writer to make use of them. As Alan Wilde explains, this "anomalously reflexive story . . . rejects the three anecdotes it encloses—anecdotes that, as told to its artist-protagonist, attribute to narrative a concern with the exceptional, the dramatic, and the consequent—in favor of the banal account of ordinary life that it itself describes and is" (118). And then there is Babel's "Guy de Maupassant," a story Carver extravagantly admires. It has a sharply realized referential subject (subsistence-level literary life in Petersburg in the winter of 1916) and a strongly rendered theme (illusion versus reality culminating in the recognition of mortality). But the story's title is the name of a famous and influential short-story writer; the narrator's seduction of the rich Jewish woman who is paying him to assist her in translating Maupassant's stories is mediated by first their discussion and then their reenactment of a seduction story by the French writer (one of three of his stories mentioned in the text); and as we have seen, the story contains memorable observations about literary style. All of these features call attention to the status of Babel's story as a self-conscious authorial construct that situates itself against a background of literary tradition and convention as well as a referential realist narrative.

Babel's story foregrounds an essential aspect of all short stories. In Sean O'Faolain's blunt formulation, "the short story is itself one vast convention" (1964, 153). In her *All Is True: The Claims and Strategies of Realist Fiction,* Lilian R. Furst elaborates on this crucial point. Realism, she insists, is simply a mode of writing like fantasy, romance, or symbolism with its own aesthetic and stylistic conventions. Like circumstantial detail and attention to contemporary social reality, *mimesis* is one of its conventions. But it is the most important: the "incorporation of the semblance of reference into the illusion-making process is a distinctive hallmark of realist narrative" (1995, 25). This *vraisemblance* is not "a literal truthfulness, in the sense of a faithful imitation of a prior reality, but rather 'the air of reality,' the verbal and textual production of an impression of truth" (173). Thus any realist short story is two-sided. On one side is a picture of life, such as that praised by Carver in Chekhov's stories: "They present, in an extraordinarily precise manner, an unparalleled account of human activity and behavior in his time; and so they are valid for all time" (*Call,* 219). But Carver, of course, is not speaking as a Russian contemporary of Chekhov or a social historian of late-nineteenth-century Russia, but rather as an engaged reader bearing witness to the self-authenticating representational power of Chekhov's narrative art. The other side, in Charles E. May's formulation, is that "in spite of all the praise for the realism of the modern short story . . . the twentieth-century version of the genre has remained highly formalized, artificial and metaphoric like its nineteenth-century antecedents." What has changed is that "a new convention of the form developed to increase the illusion of everyday reality" (1990, 73–74).

6

Concerning the question of the meaning or meanings of a short story, Flannery O'Connor is characteristically direct: "Some people have the notion that you read the story and then climb out of it into the meaning, but . . . the whole story is the meaning, because it is an experience, not an abstraction" (*MM,* 73). That is to say, what is true of a symbolic detail in realist short fiction is true of the story that contains it: the writer does not communicate meaning in the sense of a discursive formulation to be extracted from the story as a kernel from the husk. Indeed, for Carver, "the writer's job . . . is not to provide conclusions or answers. If a story answers itself, its problems and conflicts, and meets its *own* requirements, then that's enough" (*Conv,* 111). Behind this insistence one senses the authority of Chekhov, who observed that "It seems to me that the writer of fiction should not try to solve such questions as those of God, pessimism, etc. His business is but to describe those who have been speaking or thinking about God and pessimism, how, and under what circumstances. The artist should be, not the judge of his characters and their conversations, but only an unbiased witness." Of course a writer had to know his subject: "It is a bad thing if a writer tackles a subject he does not understand. . . . An artist must judge only of what he understands, his field is just as limited as that of any other specialist. . . . An artist observes, selects, guesses, combines—and this in itself presupposes a problem: unless he had set himself a problem from the very first there would be nothing to conjecture and nothing to select. . . . You are right in demanding that an artist should take an intelligent attitude to his work, but you confuse two things: *solving a problem* and *stating a problem correctly*. It is only the second that is obligatory for the artist" (1965, 58–60).

One comment of Carver's on the subject of what a story communicates/expresses is distinctly unhelpful: "In great fiction . . . there is always 'the shock of recognition' as the human significance of the work is revealed and made manifest. When in Joyce's words, its 'whatness, leaps to us from the vestment of its appearance'" (*Call,* 223). "Great fiction . . . always . . . human significance": these are sonorous fatuities. The "shock of recognition," a phrase from Melville that Edmund Wilson introduced into literary discourse, long ago became hackneyed. One is tempted to say the same of Joyce's famous description of an epiphany from *Stephen Hero,* which Carver is imperfectly remembering. Stephen Dedalus is explaining to his friend Cranly a key aspect of his aesthetic theory: "By an epiphany he meant a sudden spiritual manifestation, whether in the vulgarity of speech or of gesture or in a memorable phrase of the mind itself." It occurs when "we recognise [that the object of our scrutiny] is *that* thing which it is. Its soul, its whatness, leaps to us from the vestment of its appearance. The soul of the commonest object . . . seems to us radiant. The object achieves its epiphany" (1963, 211–13).

It is clear from the context that Carver is using the concept of epiphany in the loose, generalized sense that it has come to acquire in literary-critical discourse—a sudden moment of illumination for a character or the reader. In critical writing on short stories, the term has come to be used promiscuously and indiscriminately—for reasons suggested by Clare

Hanson: "in many 'plotless' fictions a moment of heightened awareness acts as a focus, a structural equivalent for conventional resolution of plot. Katherine Mansfield has described this development: 'If we are not to look for facts and events . . . we must be very sure of finding those central points of significance transferred to the endeavours and emotions of the human beings portrayed'" (1985, 7; Mansfield 1930, 29).[3] One might reasonably conclude that *epiphany* has become too vaguely generalized a term to be of much critical use—even in connection with Joyce's own short stories.[4]

Carver is much more helpful in other remarks concerning what a story communicates/expresses. In these comments, one can identify three components. One is "artistic delight." This is the "pleasure that's taken in reading something that's durable and made to last, as well as beautiful in and of itself. Something that throws off these sparks—a persistent and steady glow, however dim" (*Call*, 89; *Conv*, 52). The other two components are affective impact and cognitive import. At the end of a successful story, "there ought to be a unity [in the reader] of feeling and understanding. Or, if not a unity, at least a sense that the disparities of a crucial situation have

3. In her "After Epiphany: American Stories in the Postmodern Age," Miriam Marty Clark observes that "to suggest that contemporary stories do not inevitably advance toward and can no longer be read in terms of epiphany, is to challenge short-story theory at the point of greatest consensus. The epiphany is, even among critics of widely divergent opinion on other matters, almost a given" (1993, 387). For conspicuous examples of indiscriminate use, see Valerie Shaw's *The Short Story: A Critical Introduction*.

> Short stories often work towards a single moment of revelation, frequently described in Joycean terms as an epiphany, or instant of radiant insight; suddenly the fundamental secret of things is made accessible and ordinary circumstances are transfused with significance. The moment exists on the boundary between the ordinary and the mysterious, though what makes it miraculous, or even mystical, is that it fleetingly dissolves that boundary. Described as the lifting of a veil or as a moment which lays bare "the burthen of the mystery" [from Wordsworth's "Tintern Abbey"], the epiphany obviously has spiritual affinities, but its secret intimations can induce wonder without being at all otherworldly. Whether it is a shameful secret confessed, a clue brilliantly interpreted by Sherlock Holmes while Dr Watson and the reader pant to keep up with his deductions, or a moral insight freshly grasped by the central character (sometimes, but not always, seized by the reader at the same instant), many stories disclose a definite meaning, often referred to as "the point of the story." (1983, 193)

4. In 1983 Morris Beja noted of Joyce's concept of epiphany that "probably no other motif has so pervaded critical discussions of both [*Dubliners*] as a whole

been made available in a new light, and we can go on from there" (*Call*, 223). There should be "a connecting up [of story and reader] emotionally first, and then it should be an intellectual connecting up" (*Conv*, 142); "where the effects of language, situation, and insight [are] intense and total," short stories can "enlarg[e] our view of ourselves and the world": "our hearts or our intellects will have been moved off the peg just a little from where they were before" (*Call*, 220; 201–2).

In cognate terms, any fully adequate critical reading of a story involves the integration of three components: the enjoyment and contemplation of the story in and for itself; affective receptivity—response to the story's emotional content; and cognitive activity—the reflective consideration of the story's conceptual implications. The integration of all these components results in an aesthetic reading—as opposed to interpretative readings that concentrate attention on the determination (or indetermination) of meanings. Such determinations are not the function of cognitive activity alone; and sometimes the discursive formulation of the meaning of a story will be elusive, leaving the reader with a sense similar to that of the young woman in Carver's "Why Don't You Dance?" concerning an unusual episode in which she has taken part—that "There was more to it" than she can put into words; or the distraught wife's sense in the same author's "So Much Water So Close to Home" that "there is a connection to be made of these things, these events, these faces, if I can find it" (161, 234). At other times, it may even be enough to say what Lionel Trilling does in a discussion of Hemingway's "Hills Like White Elephants"—"that the meaning of a story is the *sensation* of understanding which it creates in us. . . . A story . . . is successful if it sets up in us the sensation of our having understood it" (1979, 146). It will be useful to keep this formulation in mind in connection with some of the Chekhov stories to be discussed in the following chapter.

---

and its individual stories" (3). But more recently commentators have expressed reservations concerning the use of the term. For Susan Bazargan, "The concept of epiphany has been at best a mixed blessing for Joyce. . . . At times, [epiphanies] are perceived as moments of resolution, bringing the stories to a close. But having become one of the 'rules' of reading *Dubliners*, the search for the epiphany as the sudden moment of revelation for or of the character has transformed these highly mutable stories, ironically enough, into 'idle' predictable narratives for many readers; save for the epiphanic flare-up, other interpretive lights are dimmed" (2004, 44). And see Garry Leonard's discussion of the subject in his *"Dubliners," Cambridge Companion to James Joyce*, ed. Derek Attridge, 2nd ed. (Cambridge: Cambridge University Press, 2004), 90–92.

[Chapter 1] Aesthetic Readings of Chekhov's Stories

1

In chapter 12 of Anton Chekhov's novella *Three Years*, Yulia Sergeyeva, an unhappily married young woman, attends a Moscow art exhibition. Despite her tiredness and initial indifference, she is struck by a small landscape painting:

> In the foreground a rivulet, a wooden bridge across it, a path on the other side disappearing into the dark grass, a field, then to the right a piece of forest, a bonfire nearby: it must have been a night pasture. And in the distance, the last glow of the sunset.
>
> Yulia imagined herself walking across the little bridge, then down the path further and further, and it is quiet all around, drowsy corncrakes cry, the fire flickers far ahead. And for some reason, it suddenly seemed to her that she had seen those same clouds that stretched across the red part of the sky, and the forest, and the fields long ago and many times; she felt lonely, and she wanted to walk, walk, walk down the path; and where the sunset's glow was, there rested the reflection of something unearthly, eternal. (401)

Her entry into the represented world of the painting culminates in an expansion-of-consciousness experience—a lift out of the quotidian that brings a sense of déjà vu and of contact with something big, mysterious, and seemingly timeless. It also brings a feeling of sadness, as instanced in her lonely feeling and the fact that "she kept looking at the landscape with a sad smile" (402). Yulia Sergeyevna is sufficiently struck by the painting to become its owner. It is later described as hanging in the same private room in her home that contains her icon case. But her icons are no longer displayed, because she has lost the religious faith of her early years and stopped praying to God.

The implication is that in substituting the painting for the icons, she has turned from one kind of pictorial artifact to another for spiritual nourishment. The stylized figures depicted on icons are vehicles for the transmission of preestablished doctrinal meanings. Through them, the prayerful viewer is raised to the contemplation of transcendent truths. The senses are not distracted by manifestations of the external world, because iconic convention precludes "attempts to create the illusion of real space or volume. [These] are limited to the surface of the panel and must not create an artificial impression of going beyond it. Any violation of this plane, however partial, damages the meaning of the icon" (Ouspensky and Lossky 1952, 42). The art of the landscape painting is the antithesis of this. It offers a representational illusion of the external world that engages the senses, drawing the viewer not upward but outward into its pictorial space in a way that leads to reflective sadness and a deepened awareness of the profundity of human existence.

That is to say, it is the kind of pictorial artifact that resembles the stories of Anton Chekhov. I begin with this contrast because it epitomizes my principal interest in this chapter: to distinguish between interpretative readings of Chekhov's stories—particularly Christian exegetical readings that treat his stories as if they were icons—and aesthetic readings that treat them as realist works of art.

2

In Chekhov's stories, it is more often to music than to works of visual art that characters are shown responding. Examples include the "magnificent, melancholy" singing heard from a distance in "Peasant Women" and the song, "soft, drawn out, and mournful, like weeping, and barely audible," heard by Egorushka in the second section of *The Steppe*, which at first seems to come not from a human voice but to be "the grass singing in the perishing heat, insisting that it wanted passionately to live, that it was still young and would be beautiful if it were not for the heat and drought." Both examples further suggest that Chekhov's interest in responses to musical works is connected with their ability to express sadness. So does a comment by the narrator of another story concerning "The subtle and elusive beauty of human grief, which it will take men long to understand and describe, and only music, it seems, is able to express" ("Enemies," 8), and the fiddle playing of Yakov and the title character of "Rothschild's Fiddle," the most conspicuous example among Chekhov's stories of the musical expression of grief.

But musical qualities in the stories are by no means restricted to those in which music figures. In his *History of Russian Literature,* D. S. Mirsky notes that the construction of a Chekhov story "is not a narrative construction—it might rather be called musical; not, however, in the sense that the prose is melodious, for it is not. But his method of constructing a story is akin to the method used in music. His stories are at once fluid and precise" (1949, 362).[1] And their endings sometimes have a musical resolution. An excellent example is "Gusev" (1890). Concerning Chekhov's endings, Avram Derman notes that early in his career the author "concentrated . . . all his resources to get an effect, in the most part for the emotional saturation of the reader's reaction." Then in the last decade of his creative life, beginning around 1894, Chekhov "shifted the center of gravity [of his endings] towards arousing in the reader the deepest possible mental activity." To this end, Chekhov used the device of stopping the story at the point where the central character begins to think and reflect, thus encouraging the reader to continue reflecting on his/her own (1989, 43). As we shall see, "Easter Night" (1886) is a good example of the former kind of ending, and "The Student" (1894) of the latter. "Gusev" falls between these poles. The story has definitive closure—the death and burial at sea of the title character. And it ends with a powerful effect—Chekhov's most spectacular contrasting images of temporality and transcendence—that is rich in conceptual implication.

The story's setting is the sick bay and deck of a Russian ship returning from the Far East. In the former are five dying men, including Pavel

---

1. Other commentators have also emphasized the musical qualities of Chekhov's stories. Shostakovich, for example, described Chekhov as "a very musical writer, but not in the sense that he wrote alliteratively. . . . Chekhov is musical in a deeper sense. He constructed his works in the way musical ones are constructed." He was "certain that Chekhov constructed 'The Black Monk' in sonata form; that there is an introduction, an exposition with main and secondary themes, development and so on" (1979, 223). Rosamund Bartlett explains that the sonata form, as a kind of musical construction, "is not, of course, to be confused with the specific genre of instrumental form called the sonata. Usually used by composers in the first movements of sonatas and symphonies, it . . . consist[s] of an exposition of main and secondary themes in different keys, followed by development and recapitulation, and sometimes a coda . . . . contrast, recapitulation, and yearning for closure [are] its chief hallmarks." Bartlett claims that the Russian composer's insight into Chekhov's artistic technique offers new insights into his stories (2000, 213–14). Elsewhere she mentions Wagnerian-style leitmotifs and complex patterns of associations as other musical aspects of Chekhov's musiclike technique (Bartlett 2004, xxv). In his *Chekhov's Art: A Stylistic Analysis,* Peter M. Bitsilli discusses the musical structure of *The Steppe* and "In the Ravine." Chekhov himself called his story "Fortune" (or "Happiness") "a quasi-symphony" (qtd. Conrad 1977, 98n).

Ivanych, an intellectual and political radical, and Gusev, a peasant soldier. The only events are the deaths of these characters, which are briefly noted. The center of interest is recurring pairs of contrasting images. At one point, for example, Pavel Ivanych affirms during a political rant that while most people are downtrodden, "With me it's different. I live consciously. I see everything, like an eagle or a hawk when it flies over the earth, and I understand everything. I am protest incarnate." Immediately following this, naked Chinese vendors are glimpsed through the ship's porthole standing in a boat, holding up cages of canaries and shouting "He sing! He sing!" (115–16). These are the birds that are the correct symbol of his temporal condition. In memory, Gusev is transported back to his native village, with its enormous, snow-covered pond and his brother driving his laughing children in a sleigh. But then, suddenly, "instead of a pond, a big, eyeless bull's head appears out of nowhere" and black smoke engulfs horse and sleigh (110). Remembering cold and snow in contrast to the stifling heat of the sick bay is the expression of a longing for transcendence; the menacing bull's head is an intimation of Gusev's imminent death. The same pattern recurs in a spatial rather than temporal context when Gusev "begins to suffer from some sort of yearning" and asks to be taken on deck. There, he looks up and sees "the deep sky, bright stars, peace and quiet—exactly as at home in the village." But below is the "darkness and disorder" of waves that have "no sense or pity. . . . The ship, too, has a senseless and cruel expression. This beaked monster pushes on," more frightening than an eyeless bull's head (118–19).

The last section, describing Gusev's burial at sea, contains another version of the same contrast, only this time the senseless and cruel term of the binary is given first. Sewn up in canvas, Gusev's corpse resembles a carrot or black radish. As it sinks towards the bottom of the ocean, it encounters a shark that plays with it, touches it with his jaws and teeth, and rips open the canvas to the delight of the surrounding pilot fish. Then comes the story's closing paragraph.

> And up above just then, on the side where the sun goes down, clouds are massing; one cloud resembles a triumphal arch, another a lion, a third a pair of scissors. . . . A broad green shaft comes from behind the clouds and stretches to the very middle of the sky; shortly afterwards a violet shaft lies next to it, then a golden one, then a pink one. . . . The sky turns a soft lilac. Seeing this magnificent, enchanting sky, the ocean frowns at first, but soon itself takes on such tender, joyful, passionate colors as human tongue can hardly name. (121)

Here the sea of brutal waves and shark's teeth is transformed and becomes visually one with the splendor of the sky, suggesting a balance or reconciliation of opposites. The human equivalents for these natural oppositions are death and life, temporality and transcendence. These equivalences are not recognized by the reader by means of a transference to him or her of the central character's cognitive activity, but through the "musical" arrangement of images, motifs, and themes that in this story culminates in a reflective equilibrium. No wonder, then, that on the night that he died, it was "Gusev" that the Russian composer Dmitri Shostakovich asked his wife to read aloud to him (Bartlett 2000, 205).

3

It goes without saying that in numerous Chekhov stories musical motifs are recessive and the thoughts and actions of verisimilar characters in real-life situations are dominant. But an appreciation of the musical qualities of these stories can nonetheless be essential to an integrated critical response. Two examples are the endings of "Anyuta" (1886) and "In the Cart" (1897). The title character of the first is a "small, thin brunette of about twenty-five, very pale, with meek gray eyes" who virtually never speaks (27). An impoverished seamstress, she has been kept by a succession of students. The one whose cheap furnished room she currently shares is Klochkov, a medical student studying for an examination. The unheated room is the single setting of this four-page story. As it opens, Anyuta is sitting by the window. Klochkov tells her to stand and remove her blouse so he can use her torso to assist his study of the rib cage. As she shivers and her lips, nose, and fingers turn blue with cold, he draws parallel lines on her chest with a piece of charcoal. He is interrupted by the arrival of another student, who wants to borrow Anyuta to pose for his painting of Psyche. Klochkov agrees with pleasure; but he is less pleased when, before leaving with her, his friend comments on the squalor of the room. This begins a train of thought that ends with the decision that he should immediately stop living with Anyuta and send her away. When he tells her this upon her return she says nothing, but her lips begin to tremble and then she starts to cry. He begins to feel sorry for her and, "annoyed at his own lack of character," shouts at her that she can stay another week. She silently returns to her seat by the window; he resumes studying; then "someone in the corridor shouted at the top of his voice: 'Gr-r-rigory, the samovar!'" and the story ends (30–31).

What is one to make of the selfless passivity and canine devotion of Anyuta, and her exploitation by thoughtless men who in their different ways treat her as an anatomical specimen? A *tranche de vie de Bohème?* a piece of social criticism? a story calculated to produce a pathetic response in the reader? The answer is found in two meaningful details. The first is the reference to Psyche, the loving woman in classical myth who was self-lessly devoted to her beloved (Cupid), whom she did not cease to love even when he had abandoned her. For Renato Poggioli, the activation of this allusion changes the story "into a tragic fable" and raises Anyuta from an inferior creature to one "morally far superior" to the men who exploit her (1957, 123–24). This is a lovely thought but is an incomplete reading, because it ignores the other symbolic resonance in the story—the samovar. Anyuta is both an avatar of Psyche possessing a rare purity of being and a utilitarian object passed about as the needs of men dictate. The fullest re-sponse to this story—the one that brings its elements into sharpest focus—is to hold in one's consciousness a single figure-ground image of Anyuta as both goddess and chattel. This is not a matter of churning or oscillation but of an equilibrium in which all the story's elements are held together in an aesthetic moment that mingles beauty and sadness.

"In the Cart" ends in a similar equilibrium. At one point in the story, the narrator contextualizes the social situation of the central character: "With all the work they have to do, teachers, hard-up doctors, and medical assistants never even have the consolation of thinking that they are devot-ing themselves to an ideal or helping the people, because their heads are always full of thoughts about fire-wood, getting enough to eat, bad roads, and illnesses. Life is difficult and uninteresting, and only docile carthorses like Marya Vasilievna put up with it for long" (129). The story opens in the morning with this character beginning the return trip by horse-drawn cart from town to the village of Vyazovye, where she has taught school for thir-teen years. It is a beautiful April day, but her spirits are untouched by the revivifying natural world. She senses only the unchanging rut of her pres-ent existence and has become unused to remembering the distant past when she lived a cultivated life with her family in Moscow. These memo-ries have faded as badly as has the single photograph of her mother in the damp schoolhouse. The crudity and oppressiveness of provincial exis-tence are instanced in her stop for tea in a boisterous inn and her driver Semyon's rash fording of a swollen river, which results in her provisions being soaked. When her cart passes the carriage of Khanov, a dissolute but still handsome landowner, Marya's thoughts momentarily stray to love and marriage. But this flicker of possibility is extinguished in her abiding sense of her terminally diminished self: "this life had aged her and made her coarse and unattractive; she had become awkward and clumsy, as if she were filled with lead; she was afraid of everything. . . . No one liked her, and her life was passing by miserably, without affection, without the sympathy of friends, and without any interesting acquaintances" (129).

The sun is setting splendidly as the cart finally arrives at the village. It stops at a railway crossing for an express train that is leaving the station. Then something extraordinary happens, after which the story abruptly ends:

> Here was the train. Its windows were flooded with bright light like the crosses on the church, and it hurt to look at them. On the platform at the end of one of the first-class carriages stood a lady, and Marya Vasilievna glanced at her fleetingly: it was her mother! What a resemblance! Her mother had the same luxuriant hair, the same forehead, and her head was inclined in the same way. And with amazing clarity, for the first time in all these thirteen years, she was able vividly to remember her mother and father, her brother, the apartment in Moscow, the aquarium with the little fish, and everything else down to the smallest detail; suddenly she heard the sound of the piano being played and her father's voice; she felt as if she was young, pretty, and well-dressed, in a bright, warm room, surrounded by her family as she had been then; a feeling of joy and happiness suddenly enveloped her and she pressed her palms to her temples in rapture and called out softly in supplication: "Mama!"
>
> And for no apparent reason she burst into tears. Just at that moment Khanov drove up in his coach-and-four, and when she saw him she imagined the happiness she had never had and smiled at him, nodding her head as if she was a close acquaintance and his equal, and it felt to her as if her happiness, her exultation, was reflected in the sky, in all the windows, and in the trees. No, her mother and father had never died, and she had never been a teacher; it had just been a horrible, long, bizarre dream and she had just woken up. . . .
>
> "Vasilievna, get in!"
>
> And suddenly it all vanished. The barrier was slowly rising. Shivering and numb with cold, Marya Vasilievna got into the cart. The coach-and-four crossed the tracks, and Semyon followed. The guard at the crossing took off his hat.
>
> "Here's Vyazovye. We're home." (132–33)

"In the Cart" has been highly praised, but commentators have had difficulty in substantiating their claims. H. E. Bates, for example, asserted that "the boundaries of the story gradually widen, until what appears to be a series of casual notes about a trivial journey becomes a universal tragedy of misplaced lives, of frustration. . . . Presented as individuals, [Marya and

Khanov] emerge as figures of universality. " But Bates declined the task of showing how this is done: "To explain it, to subject it to a process of analysis, is really to destroy its living tissues" (1941, 89). Irving Howe also relied on a belletristic flourish: "There is a steadfastness of vision which lifts the small bits and pieces of observation into truth, so that the fiction, in its essentials, becomes a sort of muted fable" (1994, 135). Commentators have to offer more than this if they wish to be critically useful. They also have to be accurate. Eileen Baldeshwiler, for example, asserts that in the story "symbols perform central structural functions." One of them is said to be the "difficult, painful journey by cart to the town," which is "conventionally symbolic of the entrance into one's tragic destiny" (1994, 233). But Marya is returning *from* the town to the village and has made the round trip countless times, as one is told in the story's second paragraph; and she had entered into her destiny thirteen years previously. Finally, Vladimir Kataev, in his *If Only We Could Know: An Interpretation of Chekhov,* describes the story as a late treatment of the epistemological theme (adumbrated in his title) that he traces through Chekhov's canon: "what chiefly makes [Marya] unhappy is 'not knowing why and for what reason' everything in life happens the way it does" (58). This comment is not inaccurate, but it is peripheral. It relates to the cognitive import of "In the Cart," which is a recessive consideration. What is dominant is the story's affective impact, and the principal critical task should be to elucidate this.

The climactic moment in the story is the memory vision, and one needs to be clear about its nature and status. Virginia Llewellyn Smith is not helpful in describing it as "a brief fantasy of home life" (1973, 194). It is rather an involuntary memory comparable in nature and effect to Proust's accounts of such moments in *A la recherche du temps perdu.* Indeed, Chekhov's story fully illustrates the Proustian distinction between "voluntary memory, the memory of the intellect . . . the pictures which that kind of memory shows us preserve nothing of the past itself," and involuntary memory triggered by a sense impression. Chekhov's image for the former is the faded photograph of Marya's mother, the symbol of the virtually forgotten habit memory of her early life. Her involuntary memory on the other hand has the same effect as does that of Proust's narrator when, weary and dispirited, he soaks a madeleine in a cup of tea, raises a spoonful of the mixture to his lips, and thereby releases a memory of the long-ago Sunday mornings of his childhood: "at once the vicissitudes of life had become indifferent to me, its disasters innocuous, its brevity illusory—this new sensation having had on me the effect which love has of filling me with a precious essence. . . . I had ceased now to feel mediocre, contingent, mortal. Whence could it have come to me, this all-powerful joy?" (1981, 47–48).

Marya's expansion-of-consciousness experience raises her out of the constricted existence of the past thirteen years—but only momentarily. Both literally and figuratively, she gets "in the cart" again at the story's close. Having finished the story, a reader might be tempted to wonder about the aftereffect of the memory vision: was it a sustaining recompense for loss, leaving Marya more content with the drabness and loneliness of her life; or was the contrast between vision and reality terminally demoralizing? The temptation must be resisted, because such unanswerable questions are not invited by the story, are generically inappropriate, and detract attention from the story's powerful resolution. A better question would be: what is the effect of Marya's memory vision on the reader? My answer is that the reader experiences what he/she did at the end of "Anyuta"—an equilibrium between two signifiers: the memory vision and the cart, the metonymic symbol of Marya's present and future life. These instantiations of intensity and duration, transcendence and temporality, comprise the experiential totality of her life—as Psyche and samovar do of the life of Anyuta. "In the Cart," however, is more intensely affecting than "Anyuta" because the reader of the latter can only feel *for* the title character, who does not know that she has a mythical resonance and seems too unselfconscious to realize that she is chattel. Marya Vasilievna, on the other hand, does herself experience enhancement of being and does recognize her imprisonment in duration—and through Chekhov's artistry the reader is able to feel *with* her.

4

In adult life Chekhov professed to have "no religion" and to be "not a believer." Yet during childhood, as he remarked in a letter, "I received a religious education and . . . upbringing—choir singing, reading the epistles and psalms in church, regular attendance at matins, altar boy and bell-ringing duty" (1973, 217, 374). His prose fiction gives ample evidence of Chekhov's deep knowledge of the rituals, liturgy, and customs of Russian Orthodox Christianity, and the presence of these elements in his work has long been noted by commentators. But only recently has an American trend in criticism led to "the serious study of this religious subtext in Chekhov's work," which according to Robert Louis Jackson, writing in 1993, "certainly is one of the major tasks of Chekhov criticism." When Chekhov "left the Church," Jackson asserts, "he did not step out of the Judeo-Christian world or divest himself of the culture and traditions of Russian Orthodoxy that he imbibed as a child and lived with all his life . . . . biblical and liturgical vision, imagery, and allusion permeate his art" (1993, 8–9). Julie W. de Sherbinin agrees. In "Chekhov and Christianity: The Critical Evolution" (1997), she writes that "Chekhov has left us a body of texts saturated with allusions to Christian scripture, liturgy, iconography, holidays, and saints that serve as signposts pointing to layers of meaning not immediately accessible on the surface. . . . [These] represent unturned stones that may potentially yield interpretations of great interest" (286, 294).

In my view the principal results of this critical stone-turning have been bad readings of excellent stories. A critique of the methodology of recent religious interpretations of Chekhov's stories and exemplifications of how his stories, even ones saturated with Christian allusions, are better read should begin by examining the concept of a *subtext*—the sine qua non of the critical discourse of Jackson, de Sherbinin, and the other recent commentators offering religious readings of Chekhov's stories. In Savely Senderovich's formulation in his "Towards Chekhov's Deeper Reaches" (1987), his works "possess a dimension of depth; there are in his texts deep layers of meaning not immediately apparent to an unaccustomed eye which constitute a second plane of meaning different from the surface and symbolic in nature" (2).

Before this assumption can become a useful critical tool, a number of matters need to be clarified. Is a subtext intentionally encoded in the text by the author, as some critics assume? If so, in the case of religious layering, is the intention to promote or demote Christian beliefs? The answer is not necessarily the former. Edward Wasiolek, for example, argues that the effect of the Christian references in Tolstoy's *Master and Man* is ultimately to suggest that "it is not Christian principles or faith that moves men to give themselves for others, but instincts of another sort" (1978, 188). Or should a subtext rather be considered, as it is by deconstructive critics, "a subversive or repressed text which is not consistent with the explicit text" and of which the author is "not wholly in control" (Rajan 1981, 21n). Or should religious subtexts in Chekhov be considered a matter of cultural saturation—that is, in a phrase from Northrop Frye's *The Great Code: The Bible and Literature* quoted with approbation by Jackson, a kind of "imaginative framework—a mythological universe" (Jackson 1993, 8) that, so to speak, chose Chekhov's stories as host and embedded itself in them?

These questions cannot be easily decided. On the one hand, it would be difficult to argue convincingly that Chekhov had as little creative control over his texts as the second and third possibilities presuppose. On the other, determination of intention is always a problematic undertaking. For example, de Sherbinin's attempt to resolve this question in the introduction to her *Chekhov and Russian Religious Culture: The Poetics of the Marian Paradigm* (1997) is by no means convincing. She writes that "If Chekhov's citation of Christian scripture and allusions to Christian images are taken for something akin to the 'real coin,' as they have been in several recent studies, then the question of intention is resolved by stating or intimating that these references reveal authorial sympathies in accord with the values of the sacred, of moral betterment, redemption and/or salvation" (7). But "these studies," like the ones offered in her book, presuppose the presence of the very same values she goes on to state. This means that her reasoning is circular and that nothing is resolved.

A key feature of these varieties of subtext is that they all have the same two premises. One is that a subtext is an empirical substrate of a literary work rather than a critical construction. The other is that the central critical task is the discovery and articulation of meaning through interpretative methods involving recuperation and decoding. But just because such exegetical operations can be performed on an author's works does not mean that it is good for them to be so treated. Consider, for example, the short stories in James Joyce's *Dubliners*. Joyce had as religious an upbringing as Chekhov, and his short fiction is every bit as saturated with the paraphernalia of Roman Catholic Christianity as Chekhov's is with that of Russian Orthodox Christianity. If one operated on the assumption that the Roman Catholic elements in Joyce's stories were subtextual reading keys symbolizing transcendent beliefs, one could without difficulty produce religious interpretations of the stories. But doing so would presuppose ignoring the essentials of Joyce's creative method—for example the concept of epiphany, which is the sudden realization by character or reader of the unique particularity of an object, event, or person and not their conceptual transference into a symbol of something else.

Much of the critical writing on Chekhov attests to his stories involving the communication of a mood, feeling, attitude, or emotion rather than the communication of ideas or beliefs. And other readers have given similar witness—for example, Raymond Carver: "When I read and am moved by a story of Chekhov it's similar to listening to a piece of music by Mozart and being moved by that, or being emotionally moved by something by Edith Piaf" (*Conv*, 143). Prima facie, it would follow that the kind of critical attention Chekhov's stories invite is not exclusively or even primarily interpretative. Such attention needs to be informed by a sense of how literary allusion works in a text. This device is the explicit or implicit reference to another literary text that is "sufficiently overt" to be recognized and understood by competent readers (Perri 1978, 290). It contains what Ziva Ben-Porat calls a "built-in directional signal" or "marker" that is "identifiable as an element or pattern belonging to another independent text." But I disagree with this critic when she asserts that in a literary allusion the "simultaneous activation of the two texts thus connected results in the formation of intertextual patterns whose nature cannot be predetermined" (1976, 108). Good writers exercise a large measure of control over the results of the activation. They do so by choosing one marker rather than another, by positioning the marker in one place rather than another, by the degree of explicitness of the allusion, by its proximity to other features of the text, and by the generic context. It is the critic's task not merely to identify an allusion but also to determine how the intertextual possibilities signaled by the marker should be activated. Is it a relationship of part to part, part to whole, whole to part, or whole to whole? Is the allusion a ping or a thud?

This is part of a larger consideration. Pascal observed that in reading the Bible there were two kinds of error: to interpret everything literally and to interpret everything in a spiritual sense. Something similar might be said of literary works. How is the critic to decide when to read one way and when to read the other? In the case of Christian allusions in nineteenth- and twentieth-century works, another distinction is also necessary: that between denotation and connotation. Near the end of "Tintern Abbey," for example, Wordsworth speaks directly to his sister, Dorothy, saying that he can accept the diminished present and face the uncertain future

> For thou art with me here upon the banks
> Of this fair river; thou my dearest Friend,
> My dear, dear Friend.

"For thou art with me" are the very words the speaker of the Twenty-third Psalm (in the King James version) uses to explain why, "though I walk through the valley of the shadow of death, I will fear no evil." In Wordsworth's patent allusion to the psalmist's affirmation, the denotation is changed—a human bond replaces a supernatural one—but the connotations of a fortifying and saving power are retained. And, to cite only one other example, some commentators have found comparable denotative-connotative dynamics in the allusions to the Passion and the Resurrection at the end of Tolstoy's *Death of Ivan Il'ich* (see Gutsche 1999).

Such determinations are part of the task of the aesthetic critic, which is to offer as inclusive, nuanced, and balanced an account of the artwork as he/she can. This involves considering the status of any particular of the work in relation to the ensemble of details, motifs, figures, themes, and technical and presentational features of which it is part. That is to say, an explication of any one feature of a Chekhov story should be well-tempered in relation to its other distinguishing features.

5

With this in mind, let us consider Chekhov's story "Ionych" (1898). Its opening pages foreground *poshlost* in a provincial town, epitomized by the Turkin family and focused by the title character, a callow young doctor new to the town. When the story concludes some years later, Ionych has become obese, crass, obsessed with material values, and terminally unfulfilled emotionally. In the story's second section, he goes to the town's cemetery at night for what he thinks will be a romantic rendezvous with Yekaterina, the Turkins' daughter, at the tomb of Demetti—a female singer in a touring Italian opera company who had died in the town years before. As he approaches the cemetery,

> its white stone wall appeared and a gate. In the moonlight the inscription over the gate could be read: "Behold the hour is at hand." [Ionych] went through the wicket gate, and the first thing he saw was a wide avenue lined with poplars, and white crosses and monuments on either side of it, all of them casting black shadows: all around and stretching far into the distance only black and white was visible, and the drowsy trees spread their branches over the white monuments. (239)

What is one to make of the inscription over the gate? How is it to be read? There are several possibilities. It could be considered simply as one of those inconsequential details in a realist text that give verisimilitude. But this particular detail is not like those in other Chekhov stories that Vladimir Nabokov describes as "trifles [that] are meaningless" in themselves but "all-important" in creating a "real atmosphere" (1981, 263). The inscription is more portentous than trifling, and it would be incurious of a reader not to consider what it suggests or signifies. At the referential level, there is clearly a meaning intended by those who affixed the inscription: the gate is a liminal space between ordinary human life and the mysteries of human existence. Indeed, in the solemn, black-and-white spaces inside the cemetery, Ionych has an extraordinary psychological experience. The scene seems first to offer "the promise of a quiet, beautiful, and everlasting life . . . forgiveness, sorrow, and peace." But a moment later it seems to be offering instead "the dull anguish of non-existence." Then, while waiting at the appointed tomb, Ionych's imaginings become sexualized.

Experiencing the "agony of unfulfilled desire," he begins to imagine kisses and embraces and to see eroticized marbled bodies and warm shapes in the shadows (240).

One need not end consideration of the inscription at this point, however, for what is inscribed over the gate is a literary allusion to the New Testament. Thus, at the textual rather than the referential level there is the possibility of another layer of signification. The reference is to John 5:28 and refers to Christ's prophesy of the resurrection of the dead on Judgment Day. If this allusion must be activated, I would allow myself to hear only a figural ping. The vehicle or denotation is the Christian promise of eternal life triumphing over the grave; its tenor or connotation is the promise of sexual love as a way out of the death-in-life of *poshlost*. In this reading, given the demoralizing ending of the story, the inscription becomes a comic/ironic foreshadowing of the nonappearance of the skittish and immature Yekaterina, and ultimately of the doctor's loveless nonfulfillment in life.

For Alexander Mihailovic, however, in an article in *Reading Chekhov's Text* entitled "Eschatology and Entombment in 'Ionych,'" the allusion is a resounding thud. It is nothing less than the center of "a network of Christological associations and references." Ultimately expressed in "eschatological terms" by the inscription is the potentially saving "revelation that salvation and life are a matter of choice and not the passive and cyclical inevitability of nature" (1993, 104, 113). This reading seems to me to attach far too much symbolic weight to a detail that is not the only potential signifier in the cemetery scene. More conspicuous is the tomb of the Italian opera singer, a description of which is prominently placed in the middle of Ionych's imaginings and is the hinge of the turn in his thoughts from death to sex.

Demetti's tomb, I would argue, invites one to regard Ionych's imaginings as operatic in the pejorative sense—as stagy, excessive embellishments of mortal and sexual feelings and thoughts. This suggests that as a performer, Ionych is on a par with Mr. Turkin, a tedious, boorish raconteur; with Mrs. Turkin, who loves to read aloud from her unpublished romance novels that have nothing to do with real life; with the Turkins' servant, whose one theatrical gig is a burlesque of tragic stage postures ("Die, unhappy woman"); and with Yekaterina, whose "noisy and tiresome" piano playing gives one the feeling that "she would go on hitting the keys till she had driven them into the piano" (235–36). This reading is bolstered by the abrupt ending of the cemetery scene: when the moon disappears behind a cloud "it was as though a curtain had been lowered" (246). Once offstage, when Ionych enters his carriage to return home, his only thought is that he has been putting on weight. When he proposes to Yekaterina the next day, her refusal comes in the form of a stagy declamation: "You know that I love art more than anything in the world; I love music madly, I adore it. . . . A human being must aspire to some lofty, brilliant goal and family life would bind me for ever." Ionych can hardly believe that his romantic aspirations have "petered out so stupidly, an ending worthy of a silly little play performed by some amateur company" (243). The implication is that Ionych is not a creature of free will in a redemptive drama but rather a player in a provincial melodrama with a hardwired predisposition to *poshlost*.

How is one to adjudicate the differing meanings of the inscription and to decide on its relative weight in relation to the competing signifier of the tomb? Not by asking which meaning is correct by reference to some outside-the-story criterion or to the presence of a subtext revealed by critical excavation; but rather by reference to which meaning(s) are best for the story—which make the story stronger, more richly textured and cohesive, with greater cumulative impact? In my view, the secular pings are better than the religious thud because they are compatible with each other and in aggregate make for a powerful impression. The inferior interpretation of "Ionych" is the doctrinal one because it is totalizing and precludes the other meanings, thus reducing a socially and psychologically penetrating story of a failed life to a Christian cautionary tale.

6

Several of Chekhov's stories contain features that while explicable as part of the narrative can also be read as commenting reflexively on the story and containing suggestions concerning how it should be read. Such features can be of considerable help in choosing between competing readings. As it happens, "Easter Night" and "The Student," both of which contain conspicuous reflexive elements, are also stories supersaturated with Christian motifs. Not surprisingly, both stories have recently been interpreted in the light of religious subtexts. In the former story, a first-person narrator, resembling the genteel narrator of Turgenev's *Sketches from a Hunter's Album*, recounts an incident involving socially inferior provincial persons. The story opens on a magnificent starry spring night with the narrator's account of taking a cable ferry across an expanse of swollen river to attend the midnight Easter celebrations at a monastery. The ferryman is a lay brother of the monastery named Ieronym. In conversation with him during the crossing, the narrator learns that Ieronym is deeply grieving the death that very day of his dearest friend and mentor, the deacon Nicolai, a kind and merciful soul whose sweetness of being is epitomized by his gift for composing *akathists* (special canticles sung in honor of Christ, his mother, or a saint). By the time they reach the monastery, the celebrations, including special illuminations, have begun. These are described in some detail. Dawn is breaking when the celebrations end and the narrator returns with others on the ferry, which is still being operated by the sad and weary Ieronym.

In Willa Chamberlain Axelrod's reading, the surface of "Easter Night" is ruthlessly decoded and a symbolic religious meaning laid bare. The initial crossing of the river, she asserts, "represents the Church's liturgical passage from Lent to Easter" and is thus "a metaphor for spiritual transition." Through Ieronym's account of Nicolai, "who is a Christ figure, [the narrator] is exposed to death and resurrection." The stop at the monastery "signifies the harrowing of hell, commemorated on Great Saturday." During the return crossing, the dew on Ieronym's face signifies that he "has passed over from a Lenten to a paschal disposition," while the dew on the ferry's cable transforms this version of the Cross "from a sign of death to a sign of resurrection." In the final paragraph, Ieronym "knows to look for Nicolai among the living, in the young woman with the rosy cheeks, the only passenger who specifically is wrapped in the white robe of fog." Previously a symbol of "the shroud of burial," the fog now, "in the context of the dew and resurrection . . . represents the white garments of Easter" (1993, 96–102).

What is wrong with this reading?—in my view, everything. It is an act of interpretative totalitarianism in which every particular of the surface of Chekhov's story becomes grist to a symbolic mill. In the reading I shall offer, the focal point of "Easter Night" is found not in a subtext but in the activation of the sympathetic imagination of the narrator, which invites the sympathetic emotional participation of the reader. That is to say, "Easter Night" is designed not to communicate religious meanings but to produce an intense effect. Readers will have to determine for themselves which account of "Easter Night" is stronger. But decide they must. One cannot have both readings, because Axelrod's reading involves repeated acts of conceptual transference, and the more this is done the more cerebral and the less affecting one's response to the story necessarily becomes.

At the reflexive level, the correctness of an aesthetic rather than an interpretative engagement is suggested by the implicit invitation in the text to consider similarities between the qualities of Nicolai's *akathists* as described by Ieronym and the qualities of Chekhov's "Easter Night." Nicolai possesses an extraordinary gift:

> Monks who don't understand about it reckon you only need to know the
> life of the saint you're writing to, and then follow the other akathists . . .
> but the main thing is not in the life, not in the correspondence with the
> others, but in the beauty and the sweetness. It all has to be shapely, brief,
> and thorough. . . . It has to be written so that the one who is praying will
> rejoice and weep in his heart, but shake and be in awe in his mind. (37)

At the center of the story is the loving relationship between Ieronym
and Nicolai. The quality of being of the lost loved one and of their relationship is expressed through what Ieronym tells the narrator and through
other features of the story that analogously suggest qualities of the monks'
relationship. In the private space of their friendship, "he embraced me,
stroked my head, called me tender words as if I were a little child." But
now Ieronym is "like an orphan or a widow" in a hostile environment: "in
our monastery the people are all good, kind, pious, but . . . there's no softness and delicacy in any of them." The description of the "veritable chaos"
of the public Easter celebration at the monastery—it is "filled with suffo-
cating smoke, sputtering lamps, and tumult"—is a writing large of the absence in monastery life of the softness and delicacy associated with the
being of Nicolai (38–40). Similarly, the pyrotechnical visual aspects of the
monastery's Easter celebration contrast with the silent illumination of
the stars and their reflection in the water that are the natural visual equivalents of the beauty of the *akathists.*

The *akathists* are part of the ritual and liturgical details of the Easter celebration of the central Christian belief in Christ's resurrection from the dead
and the consequent salvation of the human race. Chekhov's story is full of
these elements, and there is no question that the religious connotations
add greatly to the richness and resonance of the work and that, as Donald
Rayfield notes, they foster a "strange magical atmosphere of regeneration
and elegy" (1999, 44). But the key progression in "Easter Night" is not from
death to eternal life. It is from ordinary consciousness to expanded, sensitized consciousness—both for the narrator and the reader.

A first-person dramatized narrator helps to link the story's two set-
tings—the ferry and the monastery. But the more important function of
the narrator is to serve as the reader's surrogate and show him or her how
to respond to the story of Ieronym and Nicolai. The narrator's initial
response to hearing the former speak of his grief is dismissive. He thinks it
is "an invitation to one of those 'longanimous' soul-saving conversations
that idle and bored monks love so much" (35). And after listening to the
monk's description of the beauty of Nicolai's *akathists,* his reaction is

brusque and patronizing: "In that case, it's a pity he died . . . however, my good man, let's get moving, otherwise we'll be late" (38). But when the narrator merges with the worshippers at the monastery, he becomes "infected with the general joyous excitement," finds that he feels "unbearably pained for Ieronym," and vividly imagines how Ieronym would be feeling were he present (41).

Just after this, in the magical atmosphere of the Easter celebration an image of Nicolai himself arises in the narrator's imagination:

> God knows, perhaps if I had seen him I would have lost the image my imagination now paints for me. This sympathetic, poetic man, who came at night to call out to Ieronym and who strewed his akathists with flowers, stars, and rays of sunlight, lonely and not understood, I picture to myself as timid, pale, with gentle, meek, and sad features. In his eyes, alongside intelligence, tenderness would shine, and that barely restrained, childlike exaltation I could hear in Ieronym's voice when he quoted the akathists to me. (41–42)

This "now" is the climactic moment of "Easter Night": the shift from the past tense to the present signals a moment of expanded consciousness in which the dead Nicolai is raised to life in the imagination of the narrator—and of the reader. The raising is made possible for the narrator by an act of sympathetic imagination and for the reader by intense engagement in Chekhov's text.

In the story's final scene, we are once again on the ferry, but it is now dawn. All that remains of the monastery's luminations are heaps of black ashes. Nature seems tired and sleepy, as does the "extraordinarily sad and weary" Ieronym. What remains vivid is suggestive not of religious sublimity but of human pathos—not resurrection but human love, loss, and longing. It is the "prolonged gaze" of Ieronym seeking in a young woman's face "the soft and tender features of his deceased friend" (43).

7

"The Student" also has a paschal setting. This four-page story opens at sundown on Good Friday with a seminary student returning from a day's hunting to his impoverished family home. The weather has turned inhospitable, and he is painfully hungry. It "seem[s] to him that this sudden onset of cold violated the order and harmony of everything, that nature herself felt dismayed." Recalling the miserable living conditions of his parents and "hunching up from the cold," he begins to think "how exactly the same wind had blown" centuries before in Russia and how "there had been the same savage poverty and hunger . . . ignorance and anguish, the same surrounding emptiness and darkness, the sense of oppression" (263–64). The student is drawn by the light of an outdoor fire to where two peasant women are washing up after supper. As he warms his hands at the fire, he is reminded of a Gospel reading from Holy Week, also known to the women, the story of how on a cold night Peter had warmed his hands by a fire in a courtyard. This prompts him to recount to the women how on that occasion Peter denied three times that he knew Christ, and after the cock crowed went out and wept bitterly.

The women are strongly affected—tears roll down the cheeks of one, and the other gazes fixedly at the student with the look of "someone who is trying to suppress intense pain." Their reaction leads the student to reflect that if the woman wept, then "everything that had happened with Peter on that dreadful night had some relation to her . . . . something that had taken place nineteen centuries ago had a relation to the present." At the realization, "joy suddenly stirred in his soul. . . . The past, he thought, is connected with the present in an unbroken chain of events flowing one out of the other." As he leaves the women to cross a river by ferry and walk uphill to his village, he keeps thinking how "the truth and beauty that had guided human life" in the garden where Jesus prayed and the courtyard where Peter denied him "went on unbroken to this day." The story ends with the student feeling "an inexpressibly sweet anticipation of happiness, an unknown, mysterious happiness . . . . life seemed to him delightful, wondrous, and filled with lofty meaning" (265–66).

In an article on "The Student," Jackson immediately locates himself "on the symbolic plane of the story [where] one moves from Good Friday, the day on which Christ is crucified, to the 'feast of faith' of Easter Day." Like "Dante's confused traveler," the student is said to find himself in "a dark and threatening woods." His "paschal revelation" is signaled in the description of what he sees when he looks back upon leaving the women: "The solitary fire flickered peacefully in the darkness"—a sentence that according to Jackson "evokes John 1:5: 'And the light shineth in darkness; and the darkness comprehended it not.'" For Jackson, "the message is clear": "The passage from forest to mount, from momentary despair through communion with [the women] to a moment of spiritual transfiguration, defines the journey of both student and story." The student's walking uphill at the close of the story alludes "not only to Jesus' ascent to the mount" but also to Moses on Mount Nebo: "Like Moses, [the student] will not see the promised land on earth; like Peter, he, too, will surely experience new trials and tribulations. What is important, though, is his sustaining vision, a profoundly ethical one, of 'truth and beauty'" (1993, 127–32).

As these excerpts indicate, in Jackson's reading a religious subtext becomes a platform from which an ethical-religious message is promulgated. But Jackson misses the delicate qualifications in the story's closing sentences: that the student "was only twenty-two" and that "life seemed to him [but not necessarily to the narrator] delightful" (266). Nor does he consider the similar implications of the story's title (changed by Chekhov from "In the Evening" after the story's first appearance in print), which emphasizes the central character's youth and inexperience. The effect of these qualifications is not to undercut the affirmations of the story's concluding paragraphs but to keep the reader aware that they are a rendering of powerful subjective feelings in the consciousness of a impressionable young person of religious predisposition, and not a tapping out in code of a saving religious message.

It is also telling that Jackson fails to consider an essential feature of "The Student"—its reflexive element. It is a story about the telling of a story and its effect on its auditors and its teller. As such, it is surely reasonable to expect that any close reading of "The Student" will consider fully this reflexive dimension. Exemplary in this regard is the reading of L. M. O'Toole (unmentioned by Jackson). This critic argues that the theme of "The Student" is aesthetic rather than ethical: it is "the power of tragedy to move and inspire" through catharsis. "The choice of a Christian myth . . . is certainly vital to the story, but more in terms of setting and character than for the essential theme," which is "not the power of faith, but the power of tragedy"—the human tragedy of Peter's betrayal (1971, 46–47).

But O'Toole's structuralist "deep study of the work itself" (67) does not consider the reader's reception of the text. Is the effect of "The Student" on the reader the same as or different from the effect on the student of telling the story of Peter's betrayal to the two women and noting its effect on them? I would say the difference is that the "joy" and the sense of "truth and beauty" spoken of at the close of the story are felt experientially by the student and aesthetically by the reader. In different ways both student and reader have come into contact with one end of "an unbroken chain of events" that has been extended in one case by the student's retelling of the Gospel story and in the other by Chekhov's evocative representation of the student's experience. In this sense, what happens to the characters in the story happens to its readers. And the student's exhilaration at the end of the story is similar in kind to the reader's. How long will the student's exhilaration last? How long will the reader's? These questions are peripheral.

Concerning the former, there are several suggestions that it will be shorter-lived than he thinks it will be. Concerning the latter, all one can say is that, as with any intense experience, duration is a function of intensity. What is central is the continuing power of Chekhov's artwork to establish connections—to forge new links in a living chain that is not vertical, timeless, and sacred but horizontal, temporal, and secular.

8

In a letter to an American professor of literature concerning one of her short stories, Flannery O'Connor included a stern rebuke:

> The meaning of a story should go on expanding for the reader the more he thinks about it, but meaning cannot be captured in an interpretation. If teachers are in the habit of approaching a story as if it were a research problem for which any answer is believable so long as it is not obvious, then I think students will never learn to enjoy fiction. Too much interpretation is certainly worse than too little, and where feeling for a story is absent, theory will not supply it. (*HB*, 437)

The problem was that "many people" misunderstand how symbols function in verisimilar short fiction: "They seem to think that it is a way of saying something that [the writer is not] actually saying, and so . . . they approach it as if it were a problem in algebra. Find *x*. And when they do find or think they find this abstraction, *x*, they go off with an elaborate sense of satisfaction and the notion that they have 'understood' the story" (*MM*, 71).

The procedures of the Christian exegetes of Chekhov's stories might be described in similar terms for similar reasons. Meaning in these stories is not something to be extracted by some interpretative act involving subtexts, decoding, and conceptual transference. It is rather to be found in the sum of the reader's sympathetic engagement with the story (his or her "feeling" for the story) and his or her reflective inquiry (thinking about the story). An essential presupposition of this process is determination of what kind of story one is reading and what kind of critical treatment is best for it. Some literary texts invite interpretation in the sense of conceptual transference or decoding. Chekhov's stories invite a different kind of critical attention—not interpretative problem-solving but correct construal and an articulate aesthetic response.

[Chapter 2] Joyce's "Stories of My Childhood" and Cultural Studies

1

In his review of *Dubliners* in the August 1914 issue of the *Egoist,* Ezra Pound observed that James Joyce "gives us Dublin as it presumably is. . . . He gives us things as they are, not only for Dublin, but for every city. Erase the local names and a few specifically local allusions, and a few historic events of the past, and substitute a few different local names, allusions and events, and these stories could be retold of any town" (1954, 401). In the critical climate of almost a century later, this observation must seem to many simplistic at best. In contrast, consider this statement from the opening page of Margot Norris's *Suspicious Readings of Joyce's "Dubliners"* (2003): that with the passage of almost a century "the stories' historical and topical specificity becomes more, rather than less, necessary for interpretation" (1). At first glance, this remark might seem equally simplistic. It should go without saying that after a century, the reception of any work of realist fiction can be helpfully glossed and brought into sharper focus by social and cultural information. This is particularly true of such an historically conscious, factually grounded writer as Joyce. But what Norris actually seems to be saying is something different: that interpretative critical discourse depends on the referential context of Joyce's stories. In her cultural-studies critical model, the fictional text is regarded as a construct of social and cultural materials rather than as a self-sufficient artwork with inherent qualities. It follows that, as her title indicates, Norris privileges symptomatic readings over intentional readings.[1]

1. H. Porter Abbott usefully distinguishes between these two kinds of reading. An intentional reading "accords respect to [the] author behind the implied author"; it assumes that "a single creative sensibility lies behind the narrative [and] has selected and shaped" all of the features of the work. As Abbott notes, one advantage

Which of the two, seemingly mutually exclusive, views is correct: the one that does not consider "Dublin as it presumably is" to be a necessary reference point for understanding *Dubliners* and is essentialist in the sense of believing that works of literary art have meanings not dependent on a specific sociocultural construction; or the view maintaining that "interpretation" of Joyce's short stories is dependent upon knowledge of the particular historical and cultural situation in turn-of-the-twentieth-century Dublin? Are the former group of readers missing something necessary to a competent critical reading? Or are critics such as Norris missing something essential because of the limitations of their methodological templates? I want to consider these questions in connection with the first three stories in *Dubliners*. On the one hand, they have been admired by many readers whose knowledge of early-twentieth-century Dublin is limited to what they infer from Joyce's text. On the other hand, during the past two decades these stories, like the rest of the *Dubliners* stories, have received a great deal of attention from cultural-studies critics.[2] I offer nonsuspicious accounts of the stories, suggesting inter alia that they are less in need of interpretation in the decoding or hermeneutic sense than they have often been taken to be, and then contrast the usefulness of two recent cultural-studies readings of one of the stories.

2

Joyce described "The Sisters," "An Encounter," and "Araby" as "stories of my childhood" (qtd. Ellmann 1982, 208). All employ first-person retrospective narrators and thus stand apart in both subject and vehicle of presentation from the other *Dubliners* stories, all of which have adult protagonists and third-person narrators. Further similarities among the three suggest

---

of this kind of reading is that "it provides one of the few widely accepted standards by which interpretations can be evaluated" (2002, 95–96). In contrast a symptomatic reading, generally speaking, "reads through or past the intending author, as well as the implied author that [he/she] constructs." The narrative is seen "to express symptomatically the conditions out of which it comes" (98–102).

2. In the introductory essay to his edition of *Cultural Studies of James Joyce* (2003), R. Brandon Kersher observes that it is "striking how well the contributing strands that make up cultural studies are suited to discussions of Joyce: postcolonialism, feminism, gender studies, Marxism, cybernetics, popular/high culture investigations, and . . . the New Historicism have all been extremely visible aspects of Joyce criticism over the past twenty years or so." He estimates that "by the mid-1990s a good majority of work on Joyce arguably fell within the . . . aegis" of cultural studies (16–17).

that they make up a little trilogy (to borrow the term applied to a group of interconnected Chekhov stories) that is Joyce's "first incarnation of the artist in the process of formation" (Cixous 1972, 394) and has affinities with other portraits of the artist as child—for example, Wordsworth's two-part *Prelude* (1799) and Whitman's "There Was a Child Went Forth" (1855). But, of course, Joyce is writing realist prose fiction with an urban setting, not poetry with a natural setting, and there is correspondingly much more emphasis on the cultural milieu and socialization. In this regard, these three stories have more in common with Isaac Babel's stories of his child-hood in early-twentieth-century Odessa, which narrate stages in the child's outward movement from "a home reeking of onions and Jewish fate" ("The Awakening," 395). But all four treatments of the subject, whether in prose or verse, bear similar witness to a dictum of the narrator of one of Babel's stories: "No one in the world has a stronger response to new things than children" ("The Story of My Dovecote," 369).

Wordsworth's and Whitman's poems and Babel's stories all describe phases in the development of a sensitive and gifted child who grows up to become a creative writer whose subjects include his formative childhood experiences. These writers may be said not to succumb to the restrictions of their environment but to "fly by those nets," in Stephen Dedalus's ambiguous phrase from *A Portrait of the Artist as a Young Man* (Joyce 1992, 220), to vocational fulfillment. There is no reason not to think the same of the composite child whose formative experiences are the subject of Joyce's "stories of *my* childhood" (emphasis added). This is a crucial point. As is well known, when revising "The Sisters" (first published in the *Irish Home-stead* in 1904) for inclusion in *Dubliners,* Joyce greatly changed the opening paragraph, including the addition of the sentences containing the words *paralysis, gnomon,* and *simony.* The revised paragraph became the opening not only of "The Sisters" but also of *Dubliners,* and numerous critics have come to place considerable emphasis on the thematic implications of these words for the work as a whole. For some of them, the first word is the master key of their interpretative readings. But my subject is not *Dubliners* as a whole but its distinctive cluster of childhood stories narrated in the first person. In this context, as we shall see, the words function differently than they have been said to in the larger context of *Dubliners,* and it is neither necessary nor desirable to weight them as heavily as they have been in discussions of the larger work.[3]

3. As John Paul Riquelme notes, "the opening paragraph of 'The Sisters,' especially the first sentence, operates according to different principles [than] the rest of

A binary contrast runs through the little trilogy between the social world (the family dinner table; tedious elders; playing games; the schoolroom; the marketplace; the bazaar) and intense inner experiences of the childhood self in the process of formation. The boy in each story "remains unnamed," as Fritz Senn observes, "as though he had not yet attained a feeling of identity within the social framework" (1969, 26). "The Sisters" consists in roughly equal measure of transcriptions of adult conversation and inside views of a boy's sensitized consciousness. In "An Encounter," the contrast is nicely encapsulated in the description of the truant schoolboy's first moment of illicit freedom: "I sat up on the coping of the bridge admiring my frail canvas shoes which I had diligently pipeclayed overnight and watching the docile horses pulling a tramload of business people up the hill. All the branches of the tall trees which lined the mall were gay with little light green leaves and the sunlight slanted through them on to the water. The granite stone of the bridge was beginning to warm and I began to pat it with my hands in time to an air in my head. I was very happy" (13). In "Araby" the same contrast is powerfully condensed in the description of the soundscape of the boy and his aunt's Saturday-night marketing: "We walked through the flaring streets, jostled by drunken men and bargaining women, amid the curses of labourers, the shrill litanies of shop-boys who stood on guard by the barrels of pigs' cheeks, the nasal chanting of street-singers, who sang a *come-all-you* about O'Donovan Rossa, or a ballad about the troubles in our native land. The noises converged in a single sensation of life for me: I imagined I bore my chalice [his idealized feeling for a girl] safely through a throng of foes" (51).

Each story explores a different door of escape from Irish Catholic fate. The first leads to a mysterious region of consciousness where words, religion, and death mix; the second, via popular boys' magazines, leads to a "spirit of unruliness" and a longing for adventure (11); the third, for the child on the brink of adolescence, leads to romantic love. In each story, the desired is imaged as being found in the east: one boy has a dream in which "I felt that I had been very far away, in some land where the customs were strange—in Persia, I thought" (6); another sets out for the Pigeon House near the port of Dublin, the most eastern point in the city and the ancient place of embarkation from Ireland; and in the third story "the syllables of the word *Araby* were called to me through the silence in which my

---

the story." I am indebted to Riquelme's discussion of the relationship of narrating self to experiencing self in what he calls the three "memories of boyhood" stories (1983, 98–99).

soul luxuriated and cast an Eastern enchantment over me" (21). In each story the boy encounters an older male figure—"a repressed part of himself" according to one commentator; "a spectre of what the boy himself may one day become" according to another (Karrer 1997, 66; Senn 1969, 31). Numerous motifs and pings further interconnect and interrelate the stories: the old priest in "The Sisters" introduces the boy to "complex and mysterious" matters (6), while in "An Encounter" another peculiar old man, regarded by the boy in that story with a similar mixture of interest and revulsion, speaks of comparably strange and engaging matters. These include the desirability of having a sweetheart, a "nice young girl [with] beautiful soft hair" (16). When the boy in "Araby" is first attracted to Mangan's sister, he notices particularly the "soft rope of her hair" (20). The boy in "The Sisters" softly saying the word "paralysis" to himself while thinking of the priest's imminent death is recalled in "Araby" when the boy murmurs "O love! O love! many times" in a room of his home in which a priest had died. His secret love is figured as a hidden chalice carried through the streets, again recalling the priest of "The Sisters," whose corpse was laid out with a chalice on his breast. And as "The Sisters" ends in a dark and silent chapel, "Araby" ends in the darkness and silence of a churchlike hall.

The three stories are also linked by the use of first-person retrospective narration. In stories so narrated, there is a distinction to be made between the *I* as character and the *I* as narrator—between the younger experiencing self and the older narrating self. In some works, the temporal gap is wide, in others narrow or barely existing. But in either case it is crucial for the reader to distinguish between the two selves and gauge the distance correctly. In all three of Joyce's stories there are indications of an adult narrator recounting childhood experiences: for example, "He was shabbily dressed . . . and wore what we used to call a jerry hat with a high crown" ("An Encounter," 15); "What innumerable follies laid waste my waking and sleeping thoughts after that evening! . . . I had hardly any patience with the serious work of life" ("Araby," 21). Moreover, "An Encounter" looks very much like a story employing "the literary convention of the confession/recollection narrative" (Head 1992, 53), with a clear distance between the child protagonist and the adult narrator who is recounting a fully assimilated experience—a school-days anecdote with a nicely turned moral at the end. In a tight spot, the sensitive boy recognizes the value of his uncouth companion: "And I was penitent, for in my heart I had always despised him a little" (18).

But these features are the exception, not the rule. In the main there is little distance between narrator and protagonist in the three stories. What has been said of "Araby" is equally true of "The Sisters" and largely true of "An Encounter": "The narrator does not fulfill the conventional role of full mediation; the movement of the story is away from full mediation—the ironic distance inoperative, the evaluative stance eschewed, the narrator receding, capitulating to the experience itself" (Barney 1981, 248). Not recognizing this can lead to serious misrepresentations. For example, according to Cleanth Brooks and Robert Penn Warren in their *Understanding Fiction,* "Araby" is told "after a long lapse of time, after [the narrator] has reached maturity. This fact, it is true, is not stated in the story, but the style itself is not that of an adolescent boy . . . . the man is looking back upon the boy, detached and judicial." Having made this dubious assertion, these critics are able to posit a timeless moral. Why is the event described still significant to the older *I?* Because it is "a kind of parable of a problem which has run through later experience. The discrepancy between the real and the ideal scarcely exists for the child, but it is a constant problem, in all sorts of terms, for the adult" (1959, 192). This is specious essentialism, presupposing a character—the mature narrating self—that exists only in these critics' wishful thinking.

What is in fact the case? While "Araby," like Whitman's "There Was a Child," is written in the past tense, the only time in the story is an absolute time present. There is little distance between the two *I*'s. The narrating self does use an adult vocabulary, but there is no evidence of attitudes and values different from those of the experiencing self. And unlike the third-person narrator in some later *Dubliners* stories, he does not ironize. Indeed none of the stories in the little trilogy is written in what Joyce famously described as "a style of scrupulous meanness" that presupposes an ironic distance between narrator and protagonist (1975, 83). The older narrating self brings his considerable stylistic resources to the sympathetic depiction of the experiences of his younger self. This intensifies the reader's engagement in the story—affectively since there is no narratorial mediation between reader and protagonist, and cognitively since judgments are not supplied by the narrator nor values and norms implied.

3

In the opening paragraph of "The Sisters," the boy speculates on the imminent death of Father Flynn, the old priest who had befriended him. He ponders the priest's words, "I am not long for this world," realizing they are not idle but "true" (though true in what sense he does not say—for example, in the implication that there is another world after this one). He also broods not so much on the priest's affliction as on the word for it:

"Every night as I gazed up at the window I said softly to myself the word *paralysis*. It had always sounded strangely in my ears, like the word *gnomon* in the Euclid and the word *simony* in the Catechism. But now it sounded to me like the name of some maleficent and sinful being. It filled me with fear, and yet I longed to be nearer to it and to look upon its deadly work" (3). The boy's acute sensitivity to and interest in words are repeatedly instanced in the story: the "faints" and "worms" (distillery terms) of which old Cotter speaks; "the vague name of *Drapery*" under which the shop kept by the priest's sisters is registered; the priest's teaching him to pronounce Latin correctly and to learn the responses to the Mass. Words are for this Joycean child what aspects of the natural world are for the Wordsworthian child—they give him "a dim and undetermined sense / Of unknown modes of being" (just as the word *Araby* gives the same sense to the boy in the story of that name).

One mode of being is entered during a doze-dream into which the boy slips while he "puzzled to extract meaning" from the unfinished sentences of an adult: "I felt my soul receding into some pleasant and vicious region" in which "the heavy grey face of the paralytic" seemed smiling and trying to confess, "and I felt that I too was smiling feebly as if to absolve the simoniac of his sin" (4). Although the priest has fed his longing for mystery, this passage indicates that the boy's emotions toward him are ambivalent. He seems to have sensed the truth of the first adult comment made about the priest at the story's beginning—"there was something queer . . . there was something uncanny about him" (3). No wonder, then, that after reading the death card on the door of the priest's home, as the boy walks away "slowly along the sunny side of the street, reading all the theatrical advertisements in the shop-windows as I went," he becomes aware of a strange feeling in himself: "I found it strange that neither I nor the day seemed in a mourning mood and I felt even annoyed at discovering in myself a sensation of freedom as if I had been freed from something by his death" (5). The passage from thoughts of the deceased priest to the freedom of secular sunshine is strange to the boy but not to the reader.

After this point in narrative time, nothing more about the boy's inner life is reported. Social reality, not inner experience, is foregrounded in the long climactic scene, in which the boy and his aunt visit the house of mourning to view the corpse and then take sherry with the deceased's sisters. Kneeling at the priest's coffin, the boy reports that "I pretended to pray but I could not gather my thoughts because the old woman's mutterings distracted me. I noticed how clumsily her skirt was hooked at the back and how the heels of her cloth boots were trodden down all to one side" (7).

The ensuing conversation between the aunt and one of the sisters supplies much background information about Father Flynn, and a distinct impression of the man begins to emerge. He rose from an impoverished and uneducated background—rose too high in that the burdens and responsibilities of the priesthood had proved too heavy for one of his scrupulous and high-strung nature. (In his final days, for example, he longed to revisit the neighborhood of his childhood, but only in "one of them new-fangled carriages that makes no noise" [9]). In the story's final moments, the sister recalls a specific incident involving the breaking of a chalice that seemed to have permanently affected her brother's mind. She reports that his breakdown was revealed to others when he was found one night alone in the chapel, "sitting up by himself in the dark in his confession-box, wide-awake and laughing-like softly to himself" (10).

With this revelation, the story abruptly ends. Several critics have considered this ending in the context of the numerous hesitations, suspensions, and silences in the story and its "elliptical, evasive, sometimes mysterious" language. This has led to the conclusion that "The Sisters" is "clearly about ambiguity, about the impossibility of reaching certainty. . . . Both reader and boy are frustrated by an unsuccessful exercise in gnomic interpretation. . . . the reader, like the boy, is impelled to seek a truth he can never find" (Herring 1987, 9–11). I see the matter differently. At his family dinner table and during the conversation between his aunt and the sister, the boy tries to "extract meaning" from elliptical comments made about the deceased. So does the reader. When the reader's knowledge equals that of the sister, the story abruptly ends. It is the perfect "moment of closure" in Catherine Belsey's sense: "the point at which the events of the story become fully intelligible to the reader" (1992, 70). The reader now knows "the truth" about Father Flynn and can infer the pathos of his preceptorial relationship to the boy. But such cognitive understanding is a secondary matter. What is primary is the affective power of the image of the priest laughing-like silently in the confessional, which is intensified by the uncanny resemblance between it and the earlier description of the "pleasant and vicious region" of the boy's dozing consciousness where Father Flynn's smiling face had "begun to confess in a murmuring voice" (4). There is no narratorial registration of the boy's reaction to the image. But there hardly needs to be in that the affective impact on the reader may be taken to be the same as that experienced by the boy. In Hemingway's terms, Joyce's story has accomplished a transfer of experience to the reader. But at the same time, the reader shares with the older narrating self an understanding of the old priest's pathology.

In the context of the little trilogy, any notation at the end of "The Sisters" of the boy's reaction would have detracted from the reverberations of the climactic scenes of the next two stories, which center on other liminal moments in a sensitive boy's development and allude back to Father Flynn in the dark, silent chapel. "An Encounter," for example, becomes more resonant when read in tandem with "The Sisters." It begins with a description of boys' Wild West games and Indian battles, which have the same effect on these Irish lads as similar play did for the child Wordsworth and his Lake District contemporaries more than a century earlier: "the agency of boyish sports / . . . Impressed upon all forms the characters / Of danger or desire." Like Wordsworth, the protagonist of this story is more sensitive and inner-directed than his fellows. Under the influence of a diffused "spirit of unruliness," differences of "culture and constitution [among the boys] were waived." But the narrator is a reluctant Indian; he is struck by "the peaceful odour" of the mother of one of his friends; he several times notes his greater degree of refinement and cultivation in comparison to his peers; and it is more the solitary activity of reading stories of the Wild West than the imitative play they inspire that makes him "hunger . . . for wild sensations, for the escape which those chronicles of disorder alone seemed to offer me" (11–12).

With "a boy named Mahony," the protagonist skips school for a day's adventure. They head for the city's port—the same destination as that of the truant boy in Babel's "The Awakening." There the boy gazes at the high masts of the ships: it seems that the "geography which had been scantily dosed to me at school [was] gradually taking substance under my eyes. School and home seemed to recede from us and their influences upon us seemed to wane." But the excitement soon begins to peter out and the quotidian to reassert its grip. In Ringsend "we bought some biscuits and chocolate which we ate sedulously as we wandered through the squalid streets where the families of the fishermen live. We could find no dairy so we went into a huckster's shop and bought a bottle of raspberry lemonade each" (14). Such fare is a sad substitute for the wild sensations the boy had hungered for.

The most striking part of the day of illicit freedom begins when the boys are approached by a "queer old josser" (as Mahony calls him)—an elderly man with a cane, well-spoken but "shabbily dressed in a suit of greenish-black" (one recalls the "green faded look" of the old priest's garments in "The Sisters"). When he speaks of books and reading, and of the appropriateness of boys having sweethearts, the boy is in agreement. But there is something peculiar about the man's way of speaking—as if "his mind was slowly circling round and round in the same orbit"—that gives him a minatory aspect and makes the boy regard him with ambivalence. This intensifies when the man later changes the subject to how he would whip boys who have sweethearts "as if he were unfolding some elaborate mystery" (17). One is again reminded of the priest in "The Sisters."

His change of subject occurs after the man has excused himself to go to the end of the field in which they are sitting. "I say! Look what he's doing!" exclaims Mahony (16). But the boy does not look, and the reader is left to infer that the old man is masturbating and that the boys have been talking to a sexually disturbed and obsessive person. But it is impossible to say precisely what the disturbance is since the reader is restricted to the point of view of a child and there is no adult, like the priest's sister in the earlier story, to supply background information. What one can reasonably say is that the man seems—to the reader if not to the boy—less a sinister than a pathetic figure, a person in whom one sees "the narrowing down of a vital response to life into the confinement of a few repetitive habits and preoccupations" (Senn 1969, 30). That is to say, he is a person resembling both the priest in "The Sisters" and other characters in "An Encounter"—Father Butler, the schoolmaster who sternly admonished a boy found reading *The Apache Chief* in class instead of his Roman history textbook; and Joe Dillon, the older boy who later became a priest who had organized and always won the Wild West sieges and battles, which he celebrated with a war dance of victory. Thus, as Luke Thurston shows, "An Encounter" begins with a miniature version of its final scene: the boy had been involved "in the playing out of a fantasy scenario imposed by another . . . the alluring prospect seemingly offered by the Wild West adventures is a mere trick of perspective, whose real aim is to make room for a compulsive, meaningless repetition, always operating in favor of only one participant in the game" (2004, 22).

To where finally has the boy's door of escape led? Not into the adventurous unknown, but back to quotidian world of Mahony—a thwarting of desire that looks forward to the end of the third story. "Araby" is the most intensive and evocative of the three, resembling Babel's stories of childhood as much as it does "The Sisters" and "An Encounter." In the main, the story offers a sensory-perceptual tracking of a key phase in the passage from childhood to adolescence. Its third paragraph contains a wonderful evocation of childhood play at sunset in winter—the urban equivalent of the famous ice-skating passage in Wordsworth's *Prelude:* "The space of sky above us was the colour of ever-changing violet and towards it the lamps of the street lifted their feeble lanterns. The cold air stung us as we played till our bodies glowed. Our shouts echoed in the silent street. The career of our play brought us through the dark muddy lanes behind the houses where we ran the gantlet of the rough tribes from the cottages, to the back doors of the dark dripping gardens where odours arose from the ashpits, to the dark odorous stables where a coachman smoothed and combed the horse or shook music from the buckled harness" (19). Here, all senses save taste are in play. The passage is framed by delicate visual and aural notations: the ever-changing violet at the perceptual limit and the proximate music from the buckled harness; there are the less delicate higher-sense notations of the light of the street lamps and the boys' shouting; there are olfactory notations of ashpits and stables; and there is the haptic sting of the cold air that reaches a synesthetic intensity in the glowing of the children's bodies.

The boy's sensory profile changes with his sexual awakening—a stage anticipated in "An Encounter" when the narrator of that story notes that as a door of escape he prefers to stories of the Wild West "some American detective stories which were traversed from time to time by unkempt fierce and beautiful girls" (11). The boy in "Araby" becomes smitten with the girl known only as Mangan's sister who lives across the street. He is drawn away from the group involvement of boys' play into exclusive preoccupation with the female other. We have already noted how while shopping with his aunt the street noise around him converges into an undifferentiated "sensation of life" without, while within he cherishes an idealized religious image of the girl. The visual sense is also the organ of physical arousal both while observing the girl close-up and noting "how her dress swung as she moved her body and the soft rope of her hair tossed from side to side" and while lying on the floor of the front parlor furtively watching through the window blind for her to leave for school. "When she came out on the doorstep my heart leaped." (20).

By daylight, the garden behind the boy's house is visually drab—an apple tree, a few straggling bushes, a rusty bicycle pump. Perceived from the same window at night it becomes an acoustic space amplifying his inner feelings: "It was a dark rainy evening and there was no sound in the house. Through one of the broken panes I heard the rain impinge upon the earth, the fine incessant needles of water playing in the sodden beds. Some distant lamp or lighted window gleamed below me. I was thankful that I could see so little. All my senses seemed to desire to veil themselves and, feeling that I was about to slip from them, I pressed the palms of my hands together until they trembled, murmuring *O love! O love!* many times" (20). In this passage, darkness and silence diminish the power of eye and ear and allow for the dominance of the proprioceptive sense of touch—the palms pressed together. This suggests both the prayerful intensity of the boy's quasi-religious desire and the autoerotic intensity of sexualized feeling—a sensory-perceptual complexity recalling the "pleasant and vicious region" that the boy in "The Sisters" enters while alone in bed.

The daylight visual equivalent of this image is given three paragraphs later in the description of Mangan's sister standing on the front steps of her house: "She held one of the spikes [of the railing], bowing her head towards me. The light from the lamp opposite our door caught the white curve of her neck, lit up her hair that rested there and, falling, lit up the hand upon the railing. It fell over one side of her dress and caught the white border of a petticoat, just visible as she stood at ease" (21). In this visual rescoring of the haptic complexity of the rainy evening passage, idealizing is dominant (the pre-Raphaelite religious overtones) and the erotic recessive (the lit-up hand on the spike, the white border of the petticoat). But when the boy recalls the scene in a dark upper room of his house it is the curved neck, the hand upon the railings, and the border below the dress that are the dominant details.

When the boy first speaks with Mangan's sister, he promises to bring her something from Araby, a bazaar taking place the following weekend. But when he belatedly reaches the bazaar on Saturday night, it is already closing. In the darkness and silence of the churchlike hall, several features from earlier in the story are transmogrified and degraded: the hidden chalice that figures his love becomes the porcelain vases and flowered tea sets that are emblems of British economic colonialism (see Ehrlich 1998, 319); listening to the rain impinge on the earth becomes listening to the fall of coins on a salver; and the brief exchange of words with Mangan's sister becomes a bit of a vulgar, flirtatious exchange in English accents between a young lady and two gentleman (adults who prefigure what the boy may become). Then the hall becomes completely dark, and the story abruptly ends: "Gazing up into the darkness I saw myself as a creature driven and derided by vanity; and my eyes burned with anguish and anger" (24). Tellingly, it is a perceptual notation that concludes "Araby"—the boy's eyes are no longer the scopic channels of desire, but proprioceptive indicators of inner torment.

In one critic's reading, the story is characterized by narrative ambiguity: it "examines in a radically inconclusive way, different states of consciousness, the interaction of different timescales, and the nature of identity" (Head 1992, 53). This seems to me in its own way as unhelpful a reading as Brooks and Warren's. And for the same reason: the assumption that the reader's task is to interpret, to extract discursive meaning from a story. Such assumptions are wrongly imposed on "Araby." The story's principal concern is to represent the boy's intense feelings during a common threshold experience between childhood and adolescence. The distinction of Joyce's story is found in its delicate and evocative renderings of what it feels like to be in a state when "my body was like a harp and her words and gestures were like fingers running upon the wires" (20). The meaning of the story is that sexual awakening is an exhilarating, destabilizing, and perplexing business. This determination does not require much interpretative effort and is neither ambiguous nor inconclusive.

4

Each story in Joyce's trilogy records a phase in the development of what Whitman in "There Was a Child" called "the yearning and swelling heart" of the sensitive and imaginative child: the mystery of words, death, and adult others; "wild sensations" and the longing for adventure; the first confused stirrings of sexual desire. Each story also shows these yearnings inevitably encountering the counterpressure of the external world. In Pound's phrase, these glimpses of childhood "could be told in any town" and are hardly peculiar to turn-of-the-twentieth-century Irish Catholic Dublin. Many if not most boys have found their first exposure to the death of an adult to whom they were close a perplexing and unsettling experience; many have had an encounter with a peculiar and unwholesome adult male; and very few have not experienced a version of what Wordsworth in the fourth book of the 1805 *Prelude* calls "Slight shocks of young love-liking . . . / That mounted up like joy into the head, / And tingled through the veins."

On the other hand, these stories could not have been told by Joyce with reference to any other city than that of his own childhood. The conventions of realist narrative require *vraisemblance,* and short stories require vivid and telling detail. We know from letters written to his brother and aunt when the self-exiled Joyce was revising *Dubliners* for publication that he was scrupulous as to the factual accuracy of his representations. It is equally true that Father Flynn, his sisters, the aunt in "The Sisters," Father Butler, and the uncle in "Araby" are unmistakably Irish—even "all too Irish," to recall what Stephen Dedalus says of his father in *Ulysses* (16: 384). But literal accuracy and character typicality are less crucial to these stories than the self-authenticating "air of reality (solidity of specification)"— Henry James's phrases from "The Art of Fiction" (1:53)—created by the select details found on every page. I do not agree with Margot Norris when she speaks of "obsessive specification of turn-of-the-century shop names, streets, train stations, bridges, books, songs, personages, and events" (2003, 1) in *Dubliners*. It was not to *Dubliners* that Joyce was referring when he told Frank Budgen that he wanted "to give a picture of Dublin so complete that if the city one day suddenly disappeared from the earth it could be reconstructed out of my book" (Budgen 1960, 67–68). That book was *Ulysses*. In contrast, the degree of specification in *Dubliners* is comparatively light. A concern for the factual accuracy of details does not imply that Joyce was obsessive, indiscriminate, or profligate in his employment of them. Indeed it is hard to think of any details in the little trilogy that are not vivifying—like the notice that usually hung in the window of the sisters' shop saying *Umbrellas Re-covered;* the "musty biscuits [that] lay bleaching in windows of the grocers's shops" in Ringsend (14); the "pair of bottle-green eyes peering at me from under a twitching forehead" when the boy first looks at the face of the queer old josser (17); and the sound of "the hallstand rocking when it had received the weight of his overcoat," which alerts the boy in "Araby" to the fact that his uncle has been drinking (22).

Do the essentialist and self-authenticating qualities of Joyce's stories of childhood mean that cultural-studies discourses have nothing of value to tell us about these stories considered as works of literary art? Let us use "An Encounter" as a test case. In her suspicious reading, Norris explores "the relationship between homosexuality, homophobia, and texuality"—a choice that "may be seen as a constructivist antidote to the essentialized version of [the story's] origin promoted by Richard Ellmann [who] grounds Joyce's story in a real childhood experience." She finds that the story "performs a . . . sophisticated anatomy and enactment of the textual constructedness of the homophobic object by engaging and arousing what Eve Sedgwick calls 'homosexual panic.'" In pursuing her argument, Norris "move[s] in and out of the narration, and in and out of the text (the *text* as the narration modified by its silences and gaps, and supplemented by tacit and implicit information and knowledge)" (2003, 31–33). The result is a reading of "An Encounter" that exemplifies Norris's self-description of her readings as producing "a version so completely at odds with the manifest spirit of the stories' narration that they could be called speculative counter-narrative" (6). But I cannot see that this version has anything of value to tell a reader interested in short stories as works of literary art.

This is not the case with another cultural reading, however, that shows that asking cultural questions of literary works need not presuppose their being treated merely as cultural materials. Katherine Mullin's argument in her *James Joyce, Sexuality and Social Purity* (2003) is that Joyce's writing was deliberately and provocatively engaged with the Protestant evangelical strain of the international social-purity movement, which, as she shows, "formed part of the cultural landscape of Joyce's Dublin." She argues that several features of "An Encounter" signal its "status as a richly allusive fable about policing the reading of the young." The story opens up "questions about children, their reading, their sexuality and their punishment that the vigilance leagues attempted to close down." The queer old josser, for example, "is Joyce's particularly savage burlesque of the child-protecting social purist"; and the parallel instances of advice on reading suggest that "the respectable Father Butler and the perverse queer old josser are underneath dangerously similar. . . . Joyce's masterstroke is to make the [latter] simultaneously a child-protector and a would-be child-abuser" (22, 30, 43–48).

Mullin's fresh reading of "An Encounter" makes Norris's self-regarding discourse seem frivolous. A key difference between them is that Mullin posits authorial agency. Her reading is thus not at odds with intentional readings but rather complements them and can help make them both more robust and more nuanced.[4] Similarly, Chekhov stories such as "Peasant Women" are illuminated when placed in relation to the discourses of sexuality and morality in late-nineteenth-century Russia.[5] Such contextualizations give one a deepened sense of how much can be caught in a glimpse when the eye is that of a short-story writer of genius such as Chekhov or Joyce.

4. Another example is Vincent J. Cheng's reading of the story in his chapter on the three childhood stories in his *Joyce, Race, and Empire*. The argument of Cheng's study is that "Joyce's works house, in carefully constructed intent, a symptomatic representation of the various ideological positions on [race and colonialism] in turn-of-century Ireland—in very specific cultural and historical detail and accuracy" (1995, 9).

5. In her *The Keys to Happiness: Sex and the Search for Modernity in Fin-de-Siècle Russia*, Laura Engelstein shows how Chekhov's "Peasant Women" (1891) was "Conceived as a reply to [Tolstoy's] *The Kreutzer Sonata*. . . . It is not the power of desire that destroys human life and happiness, in Chekhov's view, but the weight of conventional norms and patriarchal relations" (1992, 238). And see the discussion of Chekhov's stories in the eighth chapter of Peter Ulf Müller's *Postlude to "The Kreutzer Sonata": Tolstoj and the Debate on Sexual Morality in Russian Literature in the 1890s* (Leiden: E. J. Brill, 1988).

[Chapter 3] Affects in Hemingway's Nick Adams Sequence

1

Between 1925 and 1933, Ernest Hemingway published fifteen short stories involving Nick Adams, the first Hemingway hero and the one who bears the closest resemblance to his creator. A number of stories narrate incidents from Nick's childhood and adolescent summers in the woods of northern Michigan—for example "Indian Camp," "The Doctor and the Doctor's Wife," and "Ten Indians," in all of which Nick's father also figures prominently. Other stories, such as "The Light of the World," "The Battler," and "The Killers," show Nick on the road in late adolescence encountering—in an argument between two prostitutes, in the pathetic relationship of a demented boxer and his black attendant, in the casualness of two hired killers and the indifference of their victim—away from home examples of the harsh actualities of the adult world. Still other stories, such as "Now I Lay Me" and "A Way You'll Never Be," are set in Italy during World War I and show the psychological repercussions of Nick's having been wounded in combat. In the final story, "Fathers and Sons," Nick is a thirty-eight-year-old writer and father remembering both his own father and Indians whom he knew in his youth in the Michigan woods.

Because of the order in which they were written and subsequently published in *In Our Time* (1925), *Men without Women* (1927), and *Winner Take Nothing* (1933), the stories about Nick were not in the sequence of his chronology and were interspersed among other stories. A number of them do gain something important through proximity to other stories not about Nick. For example, "Soldier's Home," from *In Our Time*, tells how a young man named Krebs comes home to the Midwest after the war and loses everything valuable he has gained from his overseas experiences though talking too much about them—they "lost their cool, valuable quality and then were lost themselves. . . . In this way he lost everything" (146). This story enriches one's reading of the volume's final story, "Big Two-Hearted River," which describes a solitary fishing trip Nick takes after the war and his determined efforts to hold himself together by not thinking and by immersing himself in physical activity in the perceptual present.

This arrangement, however, did a disservice to the Nick Adams stories in obscuring their interconnections and dissipating their synergies. The publication of *The Nick Adams Stories* in 1972 was therefore a welcome event, as was its inclusion of eight items of unpublished material concerning Nick—one complete and some unfinished stories, fragments, and deleted parts of published stories. But there were problems with the ordering of the materials in this volume. The fifteen previously published stories and the new items were arranged in what Philip Young, the person responsible, took to be the chronology of Nick's development. But not everyone agreed with his arrangement. In *In Our Time,* for example, the stories involving Nick, while separated by other stories, clearly seem chronologically ordered from boyhood, through adolescence, to young manhood. Thus, "The End of Something," which narrates the end of a summer romance, and "The Three-Day Blow," in which Nick and his friend Bill get drunk one afternoon and have an uproariously serious discussion about books, baseball, life, and love, precede the postwar "Big Two-Hearted River." Young himself had earlier insisted on the importance of this ordering in a critical study of Hemingway. But in *The Nick Adams Stories,* both "The End of Something" and "The Three-Day Blow" are placed after "Big Two-Hearted River" and the other post-wound stories. Young's comments on the new arrangement were understandably defensive: "matters . . . are not so simple as may first appear. Actually there isn't any completely satisfactory way to arrange them all, as readers are going to discover when they confront Nick as an adolescent veteran of the great war" (Young 1971, 6). While he did not explain his rationale for the reordering, it is clear that Young operated on the dubious principle that the chronological sequence of the Nick Adams stories was identical with that of the incidents in Hemingway's life on which they were presumed to be based.

Biographical contextualization has also informed a great deal of the critical attention that the Nick Adams stories has received—sometimes to the detriment of considering these stories as works of literary art. And some commentators have treated the group as an ur-novel, a single episodic narrative, "chronicle" (Flora 1982, 18), or "saga" (Grebstein 1973, 8), in relation to which the critical task becomes putting back into the composite text everything the author is believed to have left out. But it is the ellipses and discontinuities that sharpen and enrich these stories by generating a sense of mystery, of something happening just under the surface—without which, as Raymond Carver insists, "there simply won't be a story" (*Call*, 92). It is better to think of the Nick Adams stories as comprising a *sequence* in the sense of the term developed by M. L. Rosenthal to describe a dominant form of poetic expression in the twentieth century: a "grouping of [units], rarely uniform in pattern, that tend to interact as an organic whole . . . [the] ordering is finally lyrical, a succession of *affects*—that is, of units . . . that generate specific intensities of feeling and states of awareness" (1978, 27).[1]

I want to examine the affects in three Nick Adams stories in the light of Hemingway's comments about his fictional method, genetic materials, and their intertextual relationships to each other and to other stories in the sequence. All three center on the consciousness of Nick Adams and use strategies of omission or indirection. But they are hardly uniform in pattern, and while all employ third-person narration, the point of view differs in each. Until its closing sentence, "Indian Camp" uses objective third-person narration in recounting a series of present-time events involving

---

1. This description of a short-story sequence differs markedly from the definition of Robert M. Luscher: "the form I call the short story sequence [is] a volume of stories, collected and organized by their author, in which the reader successively realizes underlying patterns of coherence by continual modifications of his perception of pattern and theme. Within the context of the sequence, each story is thus not a completely closed formal experience" (1989, 148). Since the Nick Adams stories do not meet this first criterion, they are judged by Luscher to be not a sequence. But while an ordering of these stories according to Nick's chronology might be deemed a critical arrangement, it is not a critical construction; and had Hemingway not wanted these stories clustered and considered in terms of their intertextual relations, he surely would not have given the central character in each of them the same name and the same father.

Moreover, while seeming to privilege authorial intention, Luscher's definition in practice makes the critic the arbiter of what distinguishes a short-story sequence from a collection of miscellaneous stories. For him it is the reader/critic who "realizes," that is, constructs, the pattern of coherence that distinguishes the one from the other. That is to say, for Luscher a sequence is inescapably a critical construction. The unfortunate results of this line of thinking can be seen in a volume edited by J. Gerald Kennedy, *Modern American Short Story Sequences: Composite Fictions and Fictive Communities* (Cambridge: Cambridge University Press, 1995). Accepting Luscher's definition, the editor has included discussions of Salinger's *Nine Stories*, the title of which surely announces that it is not a sequence, as well as other volumes—for example, Henry James's *The Finer Grain* and Carver's *Cathedral*—for which the designation of sequence seems tendentious.

characters who include Nick. In "Big Two-Hearted River," the narrator has constant access to Nick's consciousness; but since Nick is determined not to think or reflect during his fishing trip, the great majority of the narration is devoted to what he senses, perceives, and does. Most of the third story, "Fathers and Sons," takes place in the consciousness of Nick; although in present time he is driving with his son through a different landscape, in his recollective free associations he is back in the northern Michigan of his boyhood and adolescence.

2

Chekhov once observed that "Novice writers usually attempt, so to speak, to 'introduce a reader to the story' and half of what they write is superfluous." The solution was for the writer to "try tearing out the first half of [the] story" (qtd. Derman 1989, 35). This is precisely what Hemingway did with the manuscript of "Indian Camp," the first of the Nick Adams stories. In its uncut version, the story opens at night with Nick in a tent during a fishing trip with his father and Uncle George. He is remembering how he had embarrassed himself the previous night when the adults had left him alone while they went night fishing. Nick had suddenly been gripped once again by the fear of dying, a condition that that had originated "a few weeks before at home, in church, [when] they had sung a hymn, 'Some day the silver cord will break.' While they were singing the hymn Nick had realized that some day he must die. It made him feel quite sick. It was the first time he had ever realized that he himself would have to die sometime" (Hemingway 1972, 14). Nick's fear intensifies until he finally fires three shots, the signal that he is in danger and his father and uncle should immediately return to the camp. We then return to present narrative time—the night after this incident. Two Indians arrive at the lake shore to fetch Nick's father, a medical doctor. Because of what had happened the previous night, his father takes Nick with him across the lake to the Indian camp. Their starting off is the point at which the final version of the story begins. The destination is a squalid shanty where a woman has been in labor for two days while her husband, badly cut by an ax, lies in the bunk over hers helplessly listening to her screams. Nick watches, or rather tries not to watch, as his father performs without anaesthetic a Caesarian section with a jackknife. But the boy is watching when his father turns his attention to the upper bunk and discovers that the husband has cut his throat from ear to ear, presumably because he has been unable to endure his wife's screams. In the story's final scene, the father rows his son back across the lake.

What is lost when Hemingway cut his story in half? In the larger context of the Nick Adams sequence, one loses the account of how, after hearing the hymn in church, Nick had become unable to sleep at night and needed a light—a motif that recurs in "Now I Lay Me," in which the adult Nick suffers from the same affliction. One also loses features that make the story seem a version of the familiar innocence-to-experience topos—the bald contrast between death apprehended through the genteel figuration of a Christian hymn and violent death seen close-up and unembellished; the irony that Nick would not have witnessed real death had he not been afraid of dying; and the concomitant twist at the story's end—the boy's fear of death paradoxically seems cured by exposure to the real thing.

But what was lost through cutting is more than compensated for by what is gained. The final version, only 1,500 words long, is a much more concise and coherent work. There is no flashback and no scene in which Nick is not present; and, until the very end, the narrator maintains a strictly reportorial outside point of view. The final version also acquires a spatial form: the frame is the two crossings of the lake—at the beginning when Nick, with his father's arm around him, is rowed across at night; and at the end when the father rows back with his son while the sun is rising. Within the frame is the shanty—the scene of instruction where Nick is exposed to the terminal human experiences of birth and death, both mediated by a steel blade. The visual center of this scene, illuminated by the father's light, is the figure of the blood-drenched suicide.

The most important result of the removal of any above-the-surface reference to Nick's *timor mortis* is intensified reader engagement. The effect is not simply what Chekhov described as that of tearing up a story's first half: "the reader understands what is going on not through any explanation on the part of the author, but rather through the movement of the story and through the conversations and actions of the characters" (qtd. Derman 1989, 35). This is simply to say that in a realist short story showing is superior to telling. It certainly is; but reader understanding per se is not what Hemingway seems principally interested in; it is rather the transfer of experience to the reader. Cutting the story removes the innocence/experience topos and replaces it with intensities of feeling and awareness—what Rosenthal calls affects. The crucial element left out of "Indian Camp" is not the discarded flashback but any present-time account of the boy's reaction to what he witnesses in the shanty. All one is told is that when his father tells him he can watch the incision being sewn up, "Nick did not watch. His curiosity had been gone for a long time." The reader's attention is further deflected from the boy's reaction by other, faintly risible, aspects of the scene—Uncle George being bitten by the Indian woman he is helping to hold down and the doctor's soon-deflated "post-operative exhilaration" (93–94).

The traumatic nature of the boy's exposure to violent birth and violent death is not foregrounded until the story's explosive final sentence. As they walk back from the shanty to the rowboat, Nick questions his father:

> "Why did he kill himself, Daddy?"
> "I don't know, Nick. He couldn't stand things, I guess."
> "Do many men kill themselves, Daddy?"
> "Not very many, Nick."
> "Do many women?"
> "Hardly ever."
> "Don't they ever?"
> "Oh, yes. They do sometimes."
> "Daddy?"
> "Yes."
> "Where did Uncle George go to?"
> "He'll turn up all right."
> "Is dying hard, Daddy?"
> "No, I think it's pretty easy, Nick. It all depends."
>
> They were seated in the boat, Nick in the stern, his father rowing. The sun was coming up over the hills. A bass jumped, making a circle in the water. Nick trailed his hand in the water. It felt warm in the sharp chill of the morning.
>
> In the early morning on the lake sitting in the stern of the boat with his father rowing, he felt quite sure that he would never die. (95)

The dialogue shows Nick wanting/not wanting to know more about what he has witnessed. But he is not really interested in statistics about suicide any more than he is in the question of where Uncle George has gone; he is preoccupied with death and with what dying is like. In the penultimate paragraph, dialogue is succeeded by natural description. It is an example of what Tony Tanner described as Hemingway's habit of registering "as it were the environmental truth of the situation, as opposed to the psychological truth of it" while at the same time intimating the latter through natural details that "seem saturated with [a] relevance" grounded in the intensity with which they are perceived (1967, 231–32). The natural description suggests release and renewal—Nick has moved from a confined space to a natural expanse, from land to water, from night to day, and from death to life—the leaping bass and the feel of air and water. But the story does not end with this paragraph, which would have been a fitting conclusion to the longer story describing the passage from one state of being to another. The final version does not move the reader thoughtfully forward but rather emotionally deeper into Nick's inner being. Hemingway said in *Death in the Afternoon* (1932) that he had long eschewed "wow" endings to stories (182). The closing sentence of "Indian Camp" is an exception. The sentence, the single inside view of Nick given in the story, is the shock that actualizes the reader's latent sense of the effect on the boy of what he has witnessed. Nick's extraordinary, contrary-to-fact conviction that he will never die indicates how traumatic the reaction has been. But the sentence does more than simply report Nick's conviction. It also intimates the subjective and therefore fallacious nature of that conviction. While the sentence describes Nick's conscious awareness, it is not restricted to his point of view and qualifies his conviction in the very act of reporting it. In early morning on a lake with his loving father taking him away from the scene of instruction, the boy can feel "quite sure" that he is part of a lasting continuum of being. But he will learn.

3

"Big Two-Hearted River" describes Nick's postwar return to northern Michigan. As he hikes uphill to the river where he will camp and fish alone, "Nick felt happy. He felt he had left everything behind, the need for thinking, the need to write, other needs" (210). Indeed, so much has been left behind that at first glance the story might appear to be a documentary narrative that could be subtitled "How to Camp and Fish: A Vade Mecum." The narrator describes in precise detail every stage in Nick's setting up camp, cooking over a fire, preparing to fish, and fishing. In a letter of March 1925 to his father, Dr. C. E. Hemingway, the son reported that "a long fishing story of mine in two parts" was soon to be published. Ernie went on to explain that he was "trying in all my stories to get the feeling of the actual life across—not to just depict life—or criticize it—but to actually make it alive. So that when you have read something by me you actually experience the thing" (Hemingway 1981, 153).

This is done in two principal ways. One is by detailing Nick's sensations at every point in the narrative: the smell of sweet fern; the sun hot on the back of his neck; the earth feeling good against his back as he lies down in the shade; the tent smelling pleasantly of canvas; the good smell of canned beans and spaghetti warming and then their good taste; the mosquito that makes a "satisfactory hiss" in the flame of his match; the rising cold shock of the stream as Nick steps into it; his boots squelchy with water as he steps out; and so on. Nick is himself a connoisseur of these moments; indeed, one of the best-known sentences in Hemingway's canon is "He did not want to rush his sensations any." The reference is to Nick's sitting on a log with his feet in the water just after the exhilaration and disappointment of hooking but failing to land a huge trout: "He sat on the logs, smoking, drying in the sun, the sun warm on his back, the river shallow ahead entering the woods, curving into the woods, shallows, light glittering, big water-smooth rocks, cedars along the bank and white birches, the logs warm in the sun, smooth to sit on, without bark, gray to the touch; slowly the feeling of disappointment left him. It went away slowly, the feeling of disappointment that came sharply after the thrill that made his shoulders ache" (227). These registrations of visual, tactile, and proprioceptive sense impressions foreground Nick's organic sensibility (to use Wordsworth's term) and the intimacy of his involvement with the natural world: the sun is warm on his back as the logs are warm in the sun; the log is felt to be smooth as the rocks are seen to be smooth. And this suggestion of synesthetic intensity is confirmed in the logs being "gray to the touch."

. This passage also exemplifies the other principal way in which the reader is helped to "actually experience the thing": the verbal renderings of visual perceptions of the landscape. It is well known that Hemingway had a model for these renderings. As he told Gertrude Stein in a letter mentioning the story, "I'm trying to do the country like Cézanne and having a hell of a time and sometimes getting it a little bit" (Hemingway 1981, 122). This attempt is also the subject of a passage in the later-deleted final section of a draft of "Big Two-Hearted River" in which Nick reflects on writing: "He, Nick, wanted to write about country so it would be there like Cézanne had done it in painting. You had to do it from inside yourself. There wasn't any trick. Nobody had ever written about country like that. He felt almost holy about it. It was deadly serious. You could do it if . . . you'd lived right with your eyes. . . . Nick, seeing how Cézanne would do the stretch of river and the swamp, stood up and stepped down into the stream. The water was cold and actual. He waded across the stream, moving in the picture" (Hemingway 1972, 239–40)

The word picture Nick sees when he wades into the stream is found in an earlier, undeleted part of the story: "On the left, where the meadow ended and the woods began, a great elm tree was uprooted. Gone over in a storm, it lay back into the woods, its roots clotted with dirt, grass growing in them, rising a solid bank beside the stream. The river cut to the edge of the uprooted tree. From where Nick stood he could see deep channels, like ruts, cut in the shallow bed of the stream by the flow of the current.

Pebbly where he stood and pebbly and full of boulders beyond; where it curved near the tree roots, the bed of the stream was marly and between the ruts of deep water green weed fronds swung in the current" (227–28). This passage shows the influence of the French painter in its solid shapes, clearly delineated lines, use of color to emphasize shape and volume, elimination of detail, and most importantly in its handling of spatial relationships. As Pavel Machotka explains: Cézanne "reoriented the elements of his pictorial space just enough to ensure that the plane of the canvas would be preserved." The viewer was made to "see objects in his paintings as existing in a deep space behind the canvas . . . and at the same time on the canvas surface itself." The effect was a greater degree of visual engagement caused by "an oscillation between these two ways of looking" (Machotka 1996, 4).[2]

But in "Big Two-Hearted River," there is more than one mode of oscillation between ways of perceiving. In later years Hemingway several times described the story as deliberately making no reference to what one would now call Nick's post-traumatic stress disorder. His fullest statement on the subject was made in 1959: "If you leave out important things or events that you know about, the story is strengthened. If you leave [out] or skip something because you do not know it, the story will be worthless. . . . 'Big Two-Hearted River' is about a boy coming home beat to the wide from a war. Beat to the wide was an earlier and possibly more severe form of beat, since those who had it were unable to comment on the condition and could not suffer that it be mentioned in their presence. So the war, all mention of the war, anything about the war, is omitted" (Hemingway 1990, 3). This and other authorial comments on the omission of any reference to the war need to be taken with a considerable grain of salt. The reason is that Hemingway's accounts of why the story is strengthened by leaving things out are mystifications, not explanations. The story is strengthened only if the reader is made to infer the under-the-surface part of the iceberg/story and to feel the tension between explicit and implicit. In the case of "Big Two-Hearted River," the inference is facilitated by the fact that either as

2. On the techniques of Cézanne's landscape paintings, see Pavel Machotka's *Cézanne: Landscape into Art.* Critical studies of the painter's influence on Hemingway include Emily Stipes Watts, *Ernest Hemingway and the Visual Arts* (Urbana: University of Illinois Press, 1971); Meyly Chin Hagemann, "Hemingway's Secret: Visual to Verbal Art," *Journal of Modern Literature* 7 (1979): 87–112; and Paul M. Hedeen, "Moving in the Picture: The Landscape Stylistics of *In Our Time,*" *Literature and Style* 18 (1985): 363–76.

the concluding story of *In Our Time*—the sixth inter-chapter of which describes Nick's being wounded during combat on the Italian front—or in its chronological place among the Nick Adams stories, the reader already has knowledge of his having been beat to the wide by his experiences in the war. In "Now I Lay Me," for example, Nick lies awake throughout the night in a room containing ranks of mulberry leaves on which silkworms are feeding. Nick is awake because he cannot sleep without a light on "ever since I had been blown up at night and felt [my soul] go out of me and go off and then come back" (363). To occupy himself, he recalls in detail past experiences—like a trout stream he had once fished and piscatorial activi- ties that include catching grasshoppers in a meadow for bait and fishing in a swamp. Thus Hemingway's story is given resonance and depth of impli- cation because the reader *does* have a sense of what is beneath the surface of Nick's consciousness.

The key point is that in the story itself this knowledge remains implicit. This point is crucial; not recognizing it has been the cause of a lot of inap- posite psychological criticism of "Big Two-Hearted River" that confuses Hemingway's biography with the Nick Adams sequence. It has also led to the following observation by Charles E. May:

> One of the most significant implications of the compactness demanded of the short story is the need to transform mere objects and events into significance. Whereas the particular can remain merely the particular in the novel, in the short story, Elizabeth Bowen suggests, "the particular must be given general significance" . . . in a short story, such as Heming- way's "Big Two-Hearted River" . . . the physical realities exist only to em- body Nick's psychic problem. . . . Nick is not concerned with surviving an external conflict but rather an internal one. In the short story the hard material outlines of the external world are inevitably transformed into the objectifications of psychic distress. Thus, at the end of Hemingway's story, Nick's refusal to go into the swamp is purely a metaphoric refusal, having nothing to do with the "real" qualities of the swamp. (May 2004, 18)

This description valorizes one of the three components of full response to the story—the cognitive—to the exclusion of the affective component. In the case of "Big Two-Hearted River" the latter, not the former, is dominant.

Consider the detailed descriptions of Nick's camp-making activities, which include the following:

> With the ax he slit off a bright slab of pine from one of the stumps and split it into pegs for the tent. He wanted them long and solid to hold

in the ground. . . . Nick tied the rope that served the tent for a ridge-pole to the trunk of one of the pine trees and pulled the tent up off the ground with the other end of the rope and tied it to the other pine. The tent hung on the rope like a canvas blanket on a clothesline. Nick poked a hole he had cut up under the back peak of the canvas and then made it a tent by pegging out the sides. He pegged the sides out taut and drove the pegs deep, hitting them down into the ground with the flat of the ax until the rope loops were buried and the canvas was drum tight. (214–15)

As Richard L. McLain has observed, each action "offers an isolated satisfaction and, simultaneously, another step toward some larger accomplishment, satisfaction, or desire." In aggregate, "the semantic pattern" in these descriptions has "a great deal in common with the function and nature of ritual involvement: agency, prescribed activity, individual accomplished fixities, stages towards some vague satisfaction of an emotional state" (1979, 74). The effect is to create in the reader the sense that what Nick is doing is being done (in Wallace Stevens's phrase) "In the predicate that there is nothing else" (Stevens 1961, 527). The termini of the story hint at this; Nick has the burnt-out town behind him and the swamp before him. In between, "He had made his camp. He was settled. Nothing could touch him. It was a good place to camp. He was there, in the good place. He was in his home where he had made it" (215).

But the hinting is crucial. For the story to resonate, the psychological level has to remain implicit, something the reader senses without conceptual transference. For example, at the beginning of the story Nick watches trout in a river "keeping themselves steady in the current with wavering fins." Soon after he notices black grasshoppers that have survived a recent fire: "These were just ordinary hoppers, but all a sooty black in color. Nick had wondered about them as he walked, without really thinking about them. Now. . . . He wondered how long they would stay that way." Since he plans to fish for trout with grasshoppers as bait, it is only to be expected that Nick is alert to their movement and condition. But the alert reader soon notices that Nick himself seems in bad shape psychologically and that he is hoping to find relief from inner pressures through immersion in the known and loved rituals of fishing. Once one notices this, the trout keeping steady by wavering and the blackened grasshoppers that have survived burning take on a symbolic suggestiveness in relation to Nick. And for the reader who remembers the description in "Now I Lay Me" of Nick's soul going out of him and then coming back, a similar suggestiveness attaches to the big trout that "shot upstream in a long angle, only his shadow marking the angle, then lost his shadow as he came through the surface of the water, caught the sun, and then, as he went back into the stream under the surface, his shadow seemed to float down the stream with the current, unresisting" (210).

"Big Two-Hearted River" itself supplies a perceptual analogy for the effect of these details: it is like looking at "the far blue hills that marked the Lake Superior height of land. [Nick] could hardly see them, faint and far away in the heat-light over the plain. If he looked too steadily they were gone. But if he only half-looked there they were, the far-off hills of the height of land" (211). This mode of oscillation between two ways of looking perfectly suggests the flickering, figure/ground quality that details in the story have, and it further suggests that their symbolic dimensions are not caused by conceptual transference but by adjustments in focalization.

There is, however, one undeniable thud in the story: the swamp that comes to preoccupy Nick. It is perfectly understandable that Nick is reluctant to fish the swamp on his first day on the river: it is arduous to traverse and frustrating "to hook big trout in places impossible to land them." But the word *swamp* is used no fewer than eight times in the space of two paragraphs that conclude portentously: "in the fast deep water, in the half light, the fishing would be tragic. In the swamp fishing was a tragic adventure. Nick did not want it" (231). No wonder that for May the swamp exists only as an objectification of psychic distress and that another commentator calls it is "an objective correlative of the unexplored depths of Nick's psyche" (Zapf 1990, 106). But this does not make the passage artistically successful. The problem is that the symbolic meaning is showcased in a way that is out of key with the employment of meaningful details elsewhere in the story. It is a violation of the principle in early Hemingway that "none of the significant things are going to have any literary signs marking them. You have to figure them out by yourself" (qtd. Svoboda 1983, 12).

What we have here, then, is the result of authorial miscalculation, not of the ineluctable dynamics of short-story conciseness. In an abrupt change in the story's modus operandi, Nick projects a symbolic meaning onto the swamp in an passage of *style indirect libre*. One might argue that Nick is using the word *tragic* loosely to mean something the opposite of *good*, the adjective often used of positive sensations earlier in the story. Even so, *tragic* inevitably has heavy connotations for the literate reader that make its employment infelicitous. It is also redundant. Without the repeated *tragic*, one could still have figured out for oneself or sensed a connection between Nick's unwillingness to fish in the swamp and his unwillingness to explore certain areas of his psyche. Consider the way the subject is introduced: "Ahead the river narrowed and went into a swamp. The river became smooth and deep and the swamp looked solid with cedar trees, their trunks close together, their branches solid. It would not be possible to walk through a swamp like that" (230–31). To cite Stevens once again: "There was that difference between the and an, / The difference between himself and no man" (1961, 255). *The* swamp is part of the river Nick is fishing; *a* swamp is an alien something with which Nick is not at one. And in the following sentences, there is the suggestion that this place has become a minatory entity located not out there but within Nick's psychic space. Finally, without the *tragic* signposting, the reader could have better sensed the delicate equivocation of the story's closing sentence: "There were plenty of days coming when he could fish the swamp" (232). This might suggest timidity or procrastination; but it might equally be taken to register Nick's incipient confidence in his ability to get a handle on his inner self.

4

In "Fathers and Sons," we return to young Nick, his father, and the Indian camp. But now it is via the reveries and memories of Nicholas Adams, a thirty-eight-year-old writer driving with his son in mid-fall through different country, presumably in the American South. Looking at the landscape, Nick begins mentally "hunting this country for quail as his father had taught him," and thus begins to think about his father and the distressing, vaguely described circumstances of his death: "he had had much bad luck. . . . He had died in a trap that he had helped only a little to set, and they had all betrayed him in their various ways" (489–90). In the context of the Nick Adams sequence, one infers that this trap involves his marriage. In "The Doctor and the Doctor's Wife," for example, Nick's father loses his temper with a man from the Indian camp who has provoked a row so he will not have to cut logs in repayment of a debt. To compose himself, Dr. Adams goes to his bedroom to clean his shotgun. There his Christian Scientist wife cautions him about losing his temper and says she does not believe his account of the row: "Dear, I don't think, I really don't think that anyone would really do a thing like that." The story ends with the father seeking out his son:

> The doctor went out on the porch. The screen door slammed behind him. He heard his wife catch her breath when the door slammed.
> "Sorry," he said, outside her window with the blinds down.
> "It's all right dear," she said.

He walked in the heat out the gate and along the path into the hemlock woods. It was cool in the woods even on such a hot day. He found
Nick sitting with his back against a tree, reading.

"Your mother wants you to come and see her," the doctor said.

"I want to go with you," Nick said.

His father looked down at him.

"All right. Come on, then," his father said. "Give me the book. I'll put
it in my pocket."

"I know where's there's black squirrels, Daddy," Nick said.

All right," said his father. "Let's go there." (102–3)

The next scene in the sequence between the doctor and his wife occurs
in Nick's early memory in "Now I Lay Me" and describes the father's discovery of his wife's deliberate burning of the Indian artifacts that are his
cherished possessions. In Nick's reverie, this memory is associated with his
earliest memory—seeing in the attic of the house where he was born "my
mother and father's wedding-cake in a tin box hanging from one of the
rafters . . . and jars of snakes and other specimens that my father had collected as a boy and preserved in alcohol, the alcohol sunken in the jars so
the backs of some of the snakes and specimens were exposed and had
turned white" (365). This memory image is rich in implication. As several
commentators have suggested, in "Now I Lay Me" there are associations
not only between Nick's psychological malaise and his having been blown
up, but also between it and both his memories of his parents and his apprehensions—registered elsewhere in the story as well as in other stories—concerning the married state.[3] Coming to "Fathers and Sons" after reading
"Now I Lay Me," the reader might well wonder whether the same disturbances will still be detectible under the surface of Nick's consciousness.

The quail are the first of a number of the signifying animals that are a
distinctive feature of "Fathers and Sons": hunting the country in his mind,
Nick is after both game and memory images of his beloved but flawed
father. Told that if quail are flushed from the wrong side, "they will come
pouring at you" (488) from their habitual cover and be difficult to shoot,
the reader might begin to wonder if the figurative hunt will be similarly

3. See especially H. Porter Abbott, 89–90, and James Phelan. The latter even finds
in "Now I Lay Me" the "implicit assumptions that (some) women are castrating
bitches and that their malevolent force is very much like that of a mortar shell
exploding in a trench. Without the analogy, the logic of the story doesn't work"
(1998, 66).

difficult—especially when Nick reflects soon after that "Now, knowing how it had all been, even remembering the earliest times before things had gone badly was not good remembering. If he wrote about it he could get rid of it. He had gotten rid of many things by writing them. But it was still too early for that. There were still too many people. So he decided to think of something else." But Nick cannot stop thinking about his father, and the narrator is just as wrong later on in the story when he reports that "Nick was all through thinking about his father" (491, 496).

We thus have a story about a writer not being able to write a story about "it"—the same unnamed something that keeps Nick from being able to stop thinking about his father. What is this "it"? For anyone familiar with Hemingway's biography, the answer is likely to be that Nick's father, like Hemingway's (whom he closely resembles physically), committed suicide —like the husband in "Indian Camp." Such a conjecture certainly adds to the intertextual connections between the two stories. But if speculation as to the referent of the pronoun is restricted to the stories in the sequence, a better inference becomes possible—better in that it is an affect, not a conjecture dependent on extra-textual information. This inference is that what Nick cannot yet get rid of has to do as much with conflicted early memories as with his father's death per se. What is crucial in engaging with the story is not what the "it" denotes, but rather what it connotes: beneath-the-surface disturbances that charge the surface narrative with suggestions of an indeterminate angst similar to what one sensed in the boy in "Indian Camp," the insomniac soldier in "Now I Lay Me," and the solitary fisherman in "Big Two-Hearted River."

Until its final two pages, the surface of "Fathers and Sons" is principally composed of a mixture of memories of Nick's father and of his first sexual experience. The story begins in present time with Nick and his son driving through a small town with traffic lights, paved roads, and heavy trees that shut out the sun and dampen the houses. In contrast, in past time there is the trail walked by Nick with bare feet over pine-needle loam, fallen logs, and cropped grass. It leads from the family cottage to the hemlock woods behind the Indian camp, "where the trees grew high before there were any branches and you walked on the brown, clean, springy-needled ground with no undergrowth and it was cool on the hottest days" (493). The cottage is associated with the father, to whom Nick is grateful for teaching him how to shoot—"it was a passion that had never slackened" (490). He particularly remembers the father's extraordinary eyesight, invaluable in hunting; he "saw as a bighorn ram or as an eagle sees, literally." But Nick is not grateful for the misinformation his father had given him about sex:

that "mashing . . . is one of the most heinous of crimes . . . that masturba-
tion produced blindness, insanity and death, while a man who went with
prostitutes would contract venereal diseases and that the thing to do was
to keep your hands off of people" (491). The son further remembers his
hatred of his father's smell and of his violent reaction when he had been
forced to wear a used suit of his father's underwear because, even though
laundered, it retained the father's smell. He further remembers that on that
occasion he had gone to the Indian camp to get rid of the odor. It is in
the other termini of the memory path traversed in the story—the hemlock
woods behind the camp—that Nick is given a hands-on introduction to
sexual experience by the Indian girl Trudy. He likes the odors associated
with her: the sweet-grass and smoke smell of the camp, and especially her
sexual smell, which is likened to the odor of "a fresh cased marten skin."
But Nick seems to like less well Trudy's postcoital question: "You think we
make a baby?" The narrator reports that "Something inside Nick had gone
a long way away"—perhaps as far away temporally as the night in the
nearby Indian camp when he was first exposed to an Indian birth and a
father's suicide.

Nick's memories culminate in two remarkable lyrical passages, one concerning his father, the other his sexual initiation with Trudy. Here is the
first of them:

> His father came back to him in the fall of the year, or in the early spring
> when there had been jacksnipe on the prairie, or when he saw shocks
> of corn, or when he saw a lake, or if he ever saw a horse and buggy, or
> when he saw, or heard, wild geese, or in a duck blind; remembering the
> time an eagle dropped through the whirling snow to strike the canvas-
> covered decoy, rising, his wings beating, the talons caught in the canvas.
> His father was with him, suddenly, in deserted orchards and new-plowed
> fields, in thickets, on small hills, or when going through dead grass, when-
> ever splitting wood or hauling water, by grist mills, cider mills and dams
> and always with open fires. (496)

These memories are a powerful recompense for the loss of his father. They
are hardly "as solemn as a funereal oration" as one commentator takes
them to be (Nakjavani 1995, 94–95); but they do have great resonance. In
this composite description, memories of Nick's father occur in moments of
sensory and perceptual intensity during the equinoctial seasons of spring
and fall in the natural setting of what Whitman called "the varied and
ample land" of the American Midwest ("When Lilacs Last in the Dooryard
Bloom'd"). At its center is a powerful figure of apotheosis: the eagle with

his talons caught in the canvas of the decoy—recalling the trap in which the eagle-eyed father had died—but nonetheless rising with beating wings.

The other memory is different. "But what were [the Indians] like to be with?' his son asks. "It's hard to say," Nick answers, and then reflects: "Could you say she did first what no one has ever done better and mention plump brown legs, flat belly, hard little breasts, well holding arms, quick searching tongue, the flat eyes, the good taste of mouth, then uncomfortably, tightly, sweetly, moistly, lovely, tightly, achingly, fully, finally, unendingly, never-endingly, never-to-endingly, suddenly ended, the great bird flown like an owl in the twilight, only it daylight in the woods and the hemlock needles stuck against your belly" (497). The answer is that you cannot say what it was like to your son, but you can vividly remember the sensory particulars of the orgasmic experience. But it is remembered as loss, not as loss-and-recompense. Nick's memories of his father are like the excitement of hunting—they do not diminish with the passage of time: "the sensation is the same and the last one is as good as the first." In contrast, the downy nocturnal bird of first sex—the antiphonal figuration of the paternal eagle—has flown into darkness forever. Thus the memory of Nick's sexual initiation ends with an *ubi sunt* lament as he recalls the "sick sweet smell [Indians] get to have. . . . They all ended the same. Long time ago good. Now no good" (498). And while there is no mention of what specifically has happened to Trudy, Nick surely knows that the pine marten is "a native animal that is trapped, killed, and flayed for the beauty of its pelt" (Beegel 1998, 97).

These two transporting passages are the climax of "Fathers and Sons." A brief conversation between Nick and his son concludes both the story and the Nick Adams sequence. The exchange becomes most resonant when read in both contexts. Nick is powerless to communicate to his son what the story powerfully communicates to the reader—a felt sense of his conflicted memories of cottage and camp, of his father and Trudy. When his son asks about his grandfather, Nick's replies are superficial and wryly evasive. In sensing what is beneath the surface, one needs to recall the concluding exchange between father and son in "Indian Camp." The phrase "the tomb of my grandfather," repeated four times by the boy who insists on visiting it, is a reminder of the paternal death that Nick is not yet ready to get rid of by writing about; and the son's innocent hope that "we won't live somewhere so that I can never go to pray at your tomb when you are dead" is a reminder, to both Nick and the reader, of Nick's own mortality—that he is no longer the boy who had felt quite sure that he would never die (488–89).

5

V. S. Pritchett remarks of stories in the tradition of Chekhov that "There are gaps and silences in 'the plotless' short story: [these are] fatally limiting if we do not detect in those stories the murmur of a containing society of other human beings" (2006, 345). Such a murmur is largely absent from the stories of Hemingway. This was Frank O'Connor's point when he observed that as a short-story writer Hemingway "is always a displaced person; he has no place to bring his treasures to" (1968, 314). And this is why the inter-story affects in the Nick Adams sequence are crucial—they supply a resonating murmur of implication that is another of the ways in which realist short stories can escape being short.

[Chapter 4] O'Connor's Christian Realism

1

In a letter of 1955 to a writer who had asked for comments on a short story, Flannery O'Connor replied: "You have to let the things in the story do the talking. . . . Let the old man go through his motions without any comment from you as author and let the things he sees make the pathetic effects. Do you know Joyce's story 'The Dead'? See how he makes the snow work in that story. Chekhov [in "Misery" or "The Lament"] makes everything work—the air, the light, the cold, the dirt, etc. Show these things and you don't have to say them." She also recommended Cleanth Brooks and Robert Penn Warren's *Understanding Fiction*, "a book that has been of invaluable help to me" (*HB*, 83–84). O'Connor, who described herself as belonging "to that literary generation whose education was in the hands of New Critics or those influenced by them" (qtd. Asals 1982, 130), was not exaggerating the influence on her of this widely influential textbook. Throughout her career, as Frederick Crews has noted, she never strayed "from the regnant creative-writing mode. Even the most impressive and original of her stories adhere to the classroom model of her day" (1992, 144).

For O'Connor, a story "is a complete dramatic action—and in good stories, the characters are shown through the action and the action is controlled through the characters, and the result of this is meaning that derives from the whole presented experience." Since the presentation is dramatic, the narration should be objective with no authorial commentary: the writer "has to do it by showing, not by saying, and by showing the concrete"; the reader is left "to make his own way amid experiences dramatically rendered and symbolically ordered" (*MM*, 90, 98, 139). The writer also had to see to it that his/her "thoughts and feeling—whatever they were—were aptly contained within [an] elected image" (qtd. Asals 1982, 130). The symbols and images had to derive from, be rooted in, the perceptual world of the story: "Fiction operates through the senses. . . . No reader who doesn't actually experience, who isn't made to feel, the story is going to believe anything the fiction writer merely tells him. The first and most obvious characteristic of fiction is that it deals with reality through what can be seen, heard, smelt, tasted, and touched" (*MM,* 91).

O'Connor's fidelity to New Critical principles was rewarded in 1959, when what has become her best-known story, "A Good Man Is Hard to Find," was included by Brooks and Warren in a new edition of their text-book. This story, however, is not only rooted in the American South; like most of her mature work in the medium, it is also informed by her religious beliefs. In O'Connor's Roman Catholic view, "the meaning of life is cen-tered in our redemption by Christ and what I see in the world I see in rela-tion to that" (*MM,* 32). Man is seen as incomplete in himself and prone to evil, although redeemable when his own actions are assisted by super-natural grace. In her self-description, she is a writer who "presents mystery through manners, grace through nature"; she works to leave the reader with "that sense of Mystery which cannot be accounted for by any human formula." O'Connor is thus a special kind of realist—a realist who sees "from the standpoint of Christian orthodoxy"—who has "the kind of vision that is able to see different levels of reality in one image or one situ-ation," including the level that has to do with "the Divine life and our par-ticipation in it" (*MM,* 153, 32, 72). Thus, at the climax of "A Good Man Is Hard to Find," according to the author, "The Misfit is touched by the Grace that comes through the old lady when she recognizes him as her child, as she has been touched by the Grace that comes through him in his particu-lar suffering" (*HB,* 389).

The entry of the divine into the human world is not an everyday occur-rence, and like a spaceship reentering the earth's atmosphere it involves a violent collision—for both her characters and the reader. "I have found," O'Connor explains, "that violence is strangely capable of returning my characters to reality and preparing them to accept their moment of grace" (*MM,* 112). Thus in "Greenleaf," the moment of grace for the central char-acter occurs while she is being gored to death by a bull. And in "A Good Man Is Hard to Find" the moment of grace for the Misfit and the old lady is preceded by the massacre of her family and is coincident with her own murder by the Misfit. His final comment on her epitomizes the linkage of violence and vision in numerous O'Connor's stories: "She would of been a good woman . . . if it had been somebody there to shoot her every minute of her life" (133). O'Connor also considers distortion and other emphatic means to be necessary for effectively communicating her vision to the reader. When you cannot assume that your audience shares the same vision, "then you have to make your vision apparent by shock—to the hard of hearing you shout, and for the almost-blind you draw large and startling figures" (*MM*, 34).

O'Connor's stories have been the subject of a great deal of critical discussion. The participants divide into a majority of Christian exegetes and a minority of secular commentators. The former write books with phrases in the titles such as "Incarnational Art," "Sacramental Art," "Religious Imagination," "Religion of the Grotesque," "Catholic Grotesque," "Language of Apocalypse," "Language of Grace," "Images of Grace," "Christian Mystery," "Christian Humanism," and "Comedy of Redemption." Concerning such works, a generalization made in 1977 by Louis D. Rubin Jr. is just as applicable three decades later: "O'Connor criticism is usually not an expression of literary taste but of theological allegiance. It concentrates upon the religious authenticity of her fiction. It is thematic, not formal criticism. As such it sidesteps or obscures so much that is central to her literary art. . . . So far as a great deal of the critical commentary . . . is concerned, one might as well be dealing with *Pilgrim's Progress* or the Book of Jeremiah" (1977, 49). Minority commentators include Rubin and Crews; a few cultural-studies critics such as Thomas Hill Schaub, whose *American Fiction in the Cold War* contains an excellent chapter on "A Good Man Is Hard to Find";[1] and the French critic André Bleikasten, who insists that "between intended meanings and completed work there is necessarily a gap. . . . O'Connor's public pronouncements on [the Christian content of] her art . . . are by no means the best guide to her fiction. As an interpreter, she was just as fallible as anyone else, and in point of fact there is much of what she has said or written about her work that is highly questionable" (1985, 139).

What no commentator of either party would disagree with is that a conspicuous feature of O'Connor's signature as a creative writer is her attempt to accommodate her Christian vision within the form and conventions of

---

1. For Schaub, "we cannot fully understand [O'Connor's] fiction unless we read it as a response to liberalism. Though her religious skepticism toward the claims of humanist rationality would seem to be essentially ahistoricist, maintaining a religious point of view is not something that one does outside a culture, but is a historical act participating in the dialogue of its time" (116). In his *Flannery O'Connor and Cold War Culture* (1993), published two years after Schaub's book, Jon Lance Bacon similarly insists on "the historical contingency of O'Connor's fiction" and the importance of placing it in the cultural and political context of her time (1).

the realist short story. Dogmatic Christian beliefs, violence, and distortion, however, are not qualities that one associates with the Chekhov to Carver tradition, and it is easy to see the point of the observation that O'Connor's accommodations make "using realism as a descriptive term for [her] fiction . . . problematic on several accounts" (Shloss 1980, 59). But it is nonetheless critically essential to read O'Connor's stories in the context of the realist short story. As she herself observes, "The form of a story gives it meaning which any other form would change, and unless [one] is able, in some degree, to apprehend the form, he will never apprehend anything else about the work, except what is extrinsic to it as literature" (*MM*, 129). Each of the nineteen stories in her two collections, *A Good Man Is Hard to Find* and *Everything That Rises Must Converge*, is a distinct literary artifact and not simply a fleshing out of an invariable doctrinal skeleton. The stories are more varied than one would guess from reading some of O'Connor's Christian commentators. And their individual excellences only come into focus when they are considered aesthetically—with due consideration given to their formal features, and with their conceptual implications considered in tandem with the story's other component parts.

The realist context is also essential for making qualitative discriminations among O'Connor's stories. Let us take "The Artificial Nigger" as an example. Mr Head, a backcountry grandfather living with his young grandson, Nelson, decides to take the boy on a day trip to Atlanta in the hope that one exposure to the big city will make him content to stay in the country for the rest of his life. But in the city they become lost, confused, and vexed with each other to the point that the older denies knowing the younger. The story's climactic moment comes six paragraphs from the end when in their wanderings they happen upon the title object—a vulgar lawn ornament in a white neighborhood. The pair "stood gazing at the artificial Negro as if they were faced with some great mystery. . . . They could both feel it dissolving their differences like an action of mercy." By the story's penultimate paragraph, the figurative action has became literal: "Mr Head . . . felt the action of mercy touch him again. . . . He stood appalled, judging himself with the thoroughness of God, while the action of mercy covered his pride like a flame and consumed it. . . . He saw that no sin was too monstrous for him to claim as his own, and since God loved in proportion as He forgave, he felt ready at that instant to enter Paradise" (269–70).

In her discussion of "The Artificial Nigger," Joyce Carol Oates correctly notes that "Since there is little to prepare us for Mr Head's vision, little to suggest that he is a man deeply immersed in Christian orthodoxy and the

Bible, this turn of mind is not very convincing." She immediately adds, however, that the story, like O'Connor's other stories generally, "is not meant to be realistic." Oates further asserts that O'Connor is the most "relentlessly 'symbolic' of writers" and that analogues to her "inwardly focused imagination" include the seventeenth-century New England Puritans and the nature sonnets of Gerard Manley Hopkins (1998, 157–60). She also cites the author herself, who says in *Mystery and Manners* that the story's title object represents the working of supernatural grace. But O'Connor's stories are "meant" to be realistic, and the figural legerdemain cum theological discourse at the end of "The Artificial Nigger" is in my view a serious blemish if not a downright embarrassment. If one trusts the tale and not the teller, the showing, not the telling, the story is accounted for by a human formula—a fissure in a relationship resolved through a serendipitous encounter—and not by the authorial imposition of supernatural grace.

2

With creative writers, it is often useful to make a distinction between beliefs and temperament or sensibility. "Don't mix-up thought-knowledge with felt-knowledge," O'Connor herself cautioned. Convictions and sensibility are not the same thing, "and, of course, you write with the sensibility" —her word for what Carver calls the particular and unmistakable signature in the work of all good writers (*HB*, 491, 201). In relation to her short stories, O'Connor's thought-knowledge or convictions must sometimes be taken with a considerable grain of salt—for example, the statement that "All my stories are about the action of grace on a character who is not very willing to support it," or this extraordinary declaration: "the meaning of a piece of fiction only begins where everything psychological and sociological has been explained" (*HB*, 275, 300)—as if these dimensions of her stories were merely husks to be stripped away to reveal the Christian kernels!

In fact a number of O'Connor's stories, including some of her finest, do not involve or intimate the bestowal of supernatural grace and require only moral/psychological and/or sociological/cultural explanation. As we saw in the first chapter, O'Connor herself provided such an explanation for "Good Country People." Another example is "A Late Encounter with the Enemy," a mordant satire on southern attitudes in which a senile old man, dressed up in a fake Confederate general's uniform and attended by his Coca-Cola guzzling grandson in a Boy Scout uniform, dies onstage during a college graduation ceremony at which his sixty-four-year-old daughter is receiving a degree that will finally qualify her to teach in the same way that she has been teaching for decades. A third example is "Everything That Rises Must Converge," the subject of which O'Connor called "a certain situation in the Southern states"—that is, racial integration (*HB*, 438). The title may be taken from the writings of a visionary Catholic theologian, but in context it refers to the social collision on a city bus of a white woman and a black woman wearing identical hideous hats. As a result of the encounter, the former dies of a heart attack while calling for the black nurse of her childhood. The focalizer of the story and its central character is her callow and conceited son, Julian, who, as his mother explains to a passenger, "just finished college last year. He wants to write but he's selling typewriters until he gets started." Julian often enters "a kind of mental bubble . . . the only place where he felt free of the general idiocy of his fellows," and he is so self-deluded as to think he is not dominated by his mother. He believes that despite "her small mind he had ended up with a large one" and that he has "cut himself emotionally free of her and could see with complete objectivity" (410–12). When the black woman wallops his mother with her pocketbook because of her patronizing manner, Julian is initially delighted: "That was your black double. . . . I hope she teaches you a lesson." But when his mother collapses and then dies, it is he who has to learn the bitter lesson of his now unaccommodated existence and his entry (in the story's last words) "into the world of guilt and sorrow" (419–20). This conclusion has been described as "a moment of grace" (Leitch 1989, 138). Doing so, however, is not good for the story: it makes the author seem a Christian Pollyanna dispensing silver linings rather than an unflinching dissector of flawed characters.

Other stories that narrate profound moral and psychological changes in their central characters make use of Christian concepts such as baptism, purification, purgatory, miracle, revelation, salvation, the Cross, and Christ-likeness. But these terms are employed for their connotations as well as their denotations and should not invariably be taken to have a literal Christian reference. A good example is "The Displaced Person." In his excellent reading, Arnold Weinstein describes the story as a "profound meditation on regionalism . . . as such it is also a meditation on history, on what binds people and what separates them, on how they define their identity. . . . It is a fierce and uncompromising story, as ferocious a critique of self-sufficiency and hardness of heart in its own way as *King Lear*. It seems to be saying that the body must be both uprooted and dismembered before the spirit can be made whole" (1993, 123, 127). In a letter, O'Connor uses Christian terms to describe the story, but she is clearly speaking connotatively (as the phrases with emphasis added indicate): "The displaced person did accomplish *a kind of* redemption, in that he destroyed the place, which was evil, and set Mrs McIntyre on the road to a new kind of suffering, [a] Purgatory *at least as* a beginning of suffering" (*HB*, 118). In the story other Christian terms are used in the same way: Mrs. McIntyre speaks better than she knows when she says of the title character that "That man is my salvation," and thinks of him as "a kind of miracle" (203, 219). But the ironic aptness of her words relates to the subsequent uprooting of her material being and not to the fate of her soul, which is still undetermined when the story ends.[2]

3

That said, it is undeniable that many of O'Connor's stories are concerned to show the operation of what she variously calls "the moment of grace," "the action of grace," "the acceptance of grace," and "the presence of grace" (*MM*, 112–47). One conspicuous feature of this effort is the frequent use of the *seems* or *as if* construction—a variant of her favorite trope, the simile. For Caroline Gordon (a New Critic) this was infelicitous. O'Connor reported to a correspondent that after a session with Gordon about her writing style, "I spent a lot of time getting *seems* and *as if* constructions out of [some page proofs]. It was like getting ticks off a dog. I was blissfully unaware of all this as I was writing . . ." (*HB*, 356). For Edward Kessler in his study *Flannery O'Connor and the Language of Apocalypse*, the constructions are a key feature of her attempt to bring together the divine and the mundane. What this critic calls her "visionary poetics . . . [her] metaphors, particularly her characteristic *as if,* release a power, often violent and threatening, that demands the death of the understanding before the reader can begin to evolve a new consciousness" (1986, 84, 75).

O'Connor herself would surely have endorsed this account of the intent of her figural additives to her stories. But distinctions and discriminations need to be made. In some cases, her imagery does unsettle the reader in ways that jog him or her loose from the referential plane of the story and

2. In Jan Nordby Gretlund's view, "The sociopolitical subtext in the long and terrifying Christian short story 'The Displaced Person' comes to rival her religious plot text in importance; for some readers the subtext may even come to dwarf the main text" (2004, 152). But this critic's determination of which plot is superior and which inferior seems based on nothing more than the majority critical view of O'Connor's fiction. On the story's own terms, the plots are surely coequal—if imperfectly synergistic.

suggest the co-presence of a religious plane. But at other times, the *seems* and *as if* construction—for Kessler "the marriage ring" uniting mystery and manners in O'Connor's fiction (52)—more resembles a toggle key enabling the former to overwrite the latter. This is a matter of considerable importance. If these constructions import an *ab extra* level of meaning into a story, they violate O'Connor's own dicta that short stories should be all showing and no telling and free of authorial comment. And the more these constructions are seen to impose a Christian meaning from without upon the referential narrative, the less value a story will tend to have for readers who do not share the author's Christian beliefs. We have already noted the slippage from figural to literal in "The Artificial Nigger." The figurative treatment of the bull in "Greenleaf" is equally problematic. The title is the name of a shiftless tenant farmer with a "large and loose" wife who lives in squalor and practices "prayer healing" (315). His upwardly mobile sons contrast with the grown but still-living-at-home sons of the central character, Mrs. May, the farm's owner. When a bull loose on her property because of Greenleaf's negligence appears in one of her dreams, the animal is eating everything on her farm and is clearly a dream symbol for her apprehensions about inferiors such as the Snopes-like Greenleaf family undermining her way of living and social position. But this human formula is overwritten by the narrator, who uses figural appliqué no fewer than four times to suggest that the loose bull is a divine figure with a hankering for her— "like some patient god come down to woo her"; "like an uncouth country suitor." With a hedge wreath ripped loose and caught in the tip of his horns, it appears that the bull lowered his head "as if to show the wreath"; and when the wreath slipped down to the base of his horns, it "looked like a menacing prickly crown"—suggesting not a pagan god but a Christ-figure (311–12).

At the end of the story, when Mrs. May is gored to death by the bull, there is another quartet of similitudes: "as if [the bull] were overjoyed to find her again"; "like a wild tormented lover"; "she had the look of a person whose sight has been suddenly restored"; "she seemed . . . to be bent over whispering some last discovery into the animal's ear" (333–34). Such cartoonish figural distortion contrasts with the one effective intimation of mystery in Mrs. May's goring. When it is reported that "one of his horns sank until it pierced her heart" one hears a resonating ping in the midst of soggy thuds: earlier in the story Mrs. May had come upon Mrs. Greenleaf writhing on the ground in the midst of a prayer healing and crying out "Oh, Jesus, stab me in the heart!" (333, 317). The ping is effective showing, requiring the reader to make the religious connection and realize the implications (including the social levelling); the similitudes are mere rhetorical *telling*.

In other stories the mix of human and divine formulae is nonsynergistic for other reasons. It is useful to remember the quotation from St Cyril of Jerusalem that is the epigraph to O'Connor's first collection of short stories: "The dragon is by the side of the road, watching those who pass. Beware lest he devour you. We go to the father of souls, but it is necessary to pass by the dragon." A number of O'Connor's stories narrate a shattering encounter with some form of dragon that brings a character to the beginning point of an accurate perception of self and his/her place in the world of being. For O'Connor this encounter is a prerequisite for a further stage of spiritual enlightenment. But that would be the subject of another story. Those culminating in an encounter with the dragon—such as "Good Country People" and "Everything That Rises Must Converge"—narrate what is essentially a moral/psychological process that does not involve supernatural grace. Sometimes, however, O'Connor adds elements to stories of self-discovery that introduce the father of souls before the dragon has been passed.

Let us return to "The Displaced Person." A conspicuous presence in this story is a peacock. It is introduced in the first sentence, and a few paragraphs later its head is said to be "drawn back as if [its] attention were fixed in the distance on something no one else could see." On its next appearance it is described as standing still "as if [it] had just come down from some sun-drenched height to be a vision for them all." Then its tail is described as resembling "a map of the universe." And when later in the story the peacock raises and spreads its tail, an old priest stands transfixed, saying, "Christ will come like that . . . The Transfiguration. . . . He came to redeem us" (194, 198, 200, 226). No reader will doubt for a moment that the peacock is a flagrant signifier and that the signified is God's providential order and man's redemption in Christ. In a letter, O'Connor tried to explain the peacock's presence in the story referentially: peacocks "might be found properly" on a farm and "I suppose all priests are addled to [a peacock] because they are priests" (*HB*, 118). But this is surely disingenuous. It is the author who is responsible for this gratuitous signifier. Unlike the masterly deployment of a signifying peacock in Carver's "Feathers" (discussed in the next chapter), O'Connor's bird is not functional on the story's literal level. It is more in the nature of a decal affixed to the narrative.

Another story with a problematic winged creature is "The Enduring Chill." The central character is Ashbury, a twenty-five-year-old failed writer and literary intellectual. Self-pitying, full of callow resentment, and stricken (so he thinks) with a fatal though undiagnosed illness, he has come home from New York to die in his despised southern home—the farm of his loving and invariably cheerful mother. In the course of the story Ashbury's illusions and self-deceptions are stripped away in a series of ironic reversals, until at the end he is left with un-illusioned self-knowledge. In a letter to his mother filling two notebooks and meant to be read after his death, she is blamed for his failures and inadequacies—his imagination, he says, had been ready to be liberated, "like a hawk from its cage" but has become "some bird you [have] domesticated, sitting huffy in its pen. . . . Woman, why did you pinion me?" He hopes that when read his indictment will give his mother "an enduring chill" (304–5); but at the end we see that it is to him that the story's title applies. Ashbury dismissively insists that the local doctor is too ignorant to treat his illness. Nonetheless, Dr. Block correctly diagnoses undulant fever contracted by drinking unpasteurized milk. (Ashbury had done so the previous summer in a bogus moment of communion with the black workers in the farm dairy.) The fever will not kill the young man, but he will continue to be affected by it and thus kept dependent on his mother and vulnerable to her good intentions—for example, her suggestion that "it would be nice if you wrote a book about down here. We need another good book like *Gone with the Wind*. . . . Put the war in it. . . . That always makes a long book." Moreover, the prognosis entails the shattering of the last of his illusions—that "his god, Art . . . was sending him Death" and that he would have "some last significant culminating experience . . . before he died" (370, 373, 378).

That is the secular plot of "The Enduring Chill." The other plot is the intrusion of supernatural grace into Ashbury's life through the intervention of the Holy Ghost (imaged as a bird). This plot is energized by comic distortion and flagrant signifying. In New York, Ashbury had heard a Jesuit priest named Father Vogle (homonym of *Vogel*, the German word for bird) introduce into an intellectual conversation the third person of the Trinity—the Holy Spirit or Holy Ghost. On the ceiling of his bedroom at the farm, directly over his head, water stains have formed in the shape not of a huffy hawk but of a fierce bird that appears to be descending with spread wings and an icicle in its beak. To annoy his mother, Ashbury asks to see a priest. Expecting an educated person like the New York Jesuit, he gets a blunt and blustery old Irish parish priest who has never heard of James Joyce but does know that "you must pray to the Holy Ghost [who] will not come until you see yourself as you are—a lazy, ignorant conceited youth!" (377).

The two plots come togther in the story's final paragraph:

The boy fell back on his pillow and stared at the ceiling. . . . The old life in him was exhausted. He awaited the coming of new. It was then that he felt the beginning of a chill, a chill so peculiar, so light, that it was like a warm ripple across a deep sea of cold. His breath came short. The fierce bird which through the years of his childhood and the days of his illness had been poised over his head, waiting mysteriously, appeared all at once to be in motion. Ashbury blanched and the last film of illusion was torn as if by a whirlwind from his eyes. He saw that for the rest of his days, frail, racked, but enduring, he would live in the face of a purifying terror. A feeble cry, a last impossible protest escaped him. But the Holy Ghost, emblazoned in ice instead of fire, continued, implacable, to descend. (382)

For Kessler this ending is unsuccessful because meaning is encapsulated "into a theological concept. . . . By directly naming the Holy Ghost, [O'Connor] diminishes his power in fiction" (1986, 128, 131). In my view, the problem with "The Enduring Chill" is not that the religious meaning is made too explicit. It would not make any real difference if the last sentence were changed to read: "But it seemed to him that the bird-shaped water stain continued to descend." As O'Connor eventually came to realize, the problem was her premature introduction of the supernatural: "The Holy Ghost came too fast. . . . It's not so much a story of conversion [spiritual] as of self-knowledge [moral/psychological], which I suppose has to be the first step in conversion. You can't tell about conversion until you live with it a while." That is to say, at the end of his story, Ashbury is in exactly the same state of being as Julian at the end of "Everything That Rises Must Converge." He may now be at last open to the action of grace, but that is material for another story—or for a more extended treatment of the subject. O'Connor herself thought that the story might go better as the first chapter of "a comic novel of no mean proportions" (*HB*, 261, 299).

4

In contrast, the mixture of mystery and manners is just right in another story featuring the third person of the Trinity. "A Temple of the Holy Ghost" is the only one of O'Connor's stories to have as its subject the religious experience of a Roman Catholic. She is a twelve-year-old girl who believes in the Holy Ghost, a presence who is consequently grounded in the represented world of the story. Two slightly older girls from a Catholic boarding school are spending the weekend at the home of the girl and her mother. They frivolously refer to themselves as Temple One and Temple

Two, explaining while giggling that Sister Perpetua had told their class that should a young man misbehave with them in the back of an automobile, they were to say, "Stop, sir! I am a Temple of the Holy Ghost." But the story's protagonist takes this designation seriously, even if self-referentially: saying to herself that she is a temple of the Holy Ghost makes her "feel as if somebody had given her a present." The older girls double-date with two local Protestant boys; they entertain the girls with a hillbilly hymn about having found a friend in Jesus: "He's everything to me, / He's the lily of the valley, / He's the One who set me free" (238, 240). They respond by singing the Latin hymn "Tantum Ergo," which closes with a reference to the Holy Ghost.

The foursome attend a fair, and when the girls return they tell the protagonist about an hermaphrodite seen in the freak show. She is puzzled as to the anatomy of the "it" that was "a man and a woman both," and later while going to sleep tries to picture the tent with the freak exhibiting itself. Imagining a churchlike atmosphere, she recalls being told that the freak accepted its condition, saying, "God made me thisaway and I don't dispute hit," and then imagines the freak addressing the crowd like a preacher: "Raise yourself up. A temple of the Holy Ghost. You! You are God's temple, don't you know? Don't you know? God's Spirit has a dwelling in you, don't you know?" The next day at Benediction, the girl has a revelation that is the climax of the story. As the host is raised and the "Tantum Ergo" sung, her venial thoughts recede, and "she began to realize that she was in the presence of God." She begins to ask mechanically that God "Hep me not to be so mean. . . . Hep me not to give her [mother] so much sass. Hep me not to talk like I do." But then the girl's mind begins "to get quiet and then empty," and when the priest raises the monstrance containing the Host she finds herself thinking of the tent at the fair and the freak saying, "I don't dispute hit. This is the way He wanted me to be" (246, 248).

The implication is that the Holy Ghost is indwelling in the freak just as in the Host and that the girl's previously ungrounded and self-referential supernatural beliefs have been actualized through vicarious identification with the hermaphrodite. And, as Sally Fitzgerald shows in her excellent analysis of the story, there are other implications relating to purity and sexuality. If the freak is a temple of the Holy Ghost, it is also a Christlike lily of the valley. Fitzgerald also suggests that the girl can be read as a figure for the adult author. The story was written shortly after O'Connor learned of her own disfiguring and incurable condition, lupus, "which she sometimes described to her friends in freakish terms" and which cut her off from normal life and its possible fulfillments (1981–82, 431). This adds a resonance to the story similar to that added to Chekhov's last stories by his impending death from consumption—"The Bishop," for example, in which the dying title character tries to bring together the threads of his life, and "The Fiancée," which concludes with the report of the death of the story's tubercular preceptor figure.

In "A Temple of the Holy Ghost," then, mystery and manners are in a synergistic relationship. But I would hesitate to call it one of O'Connor's finest stories, despite its fulfilling the criteria of both Weinstein, who judges her most remarkable stories to be those that "maintain a perfect balance between mimetic reporting and spiritual event" (1993, 115), and Crews, who considers the finest stories to be those in which "'mystery,' as she called it, drastically intrudes on the mundane without requiring us either to embrace a dogma or to suspend our belief in naturalistic causation" (1992, 161). Why? Because the story is a little too tidy and textbook perfect. On its last page, for example, two signifying moments click the story shut by intimating the aftermath of revelation for the girl. Leaving the church, a big nun vigorously embraces her, "mashing the side of her face into the crucifix hitched onto her belt." And in the story's closing sentence, the sun on the horizon "was a huge red ball like an elevated Host drenched in blood" and leaves "a line in the sky like a red clay road hanging over the trees" (248). These neatly deployed details suggest the cold-blooded carpentry of the well-made story. As O'Connor explained in a letter: "The point is of course in the resignation to suffering, which is one of the fruits of the Holy Ghost" (1988, 925). Her "of course" is of course the problem.

I have the same hesitation concerning another excellent story. In "Revelation," the dragon that the central character has to pass by is a Wellesley undergraduate with mental problems. She is O'Connor's version of the mad truth-teller figure who appears in several places in the American fiction of the early 1960s (for example in Richard Yates's *Revolutionary Road* and Ken Kesey's *One Flew over the Cuckoo's Nest*) as the excoriator of middle-class complacency and mediocrity. This young woman hurls a book entitled *Human Development* across the waiting room of the doctor's office in which the first two-thirds of the story is set. It is aimed at the story's central character, Mrs. Turpin, and strikes her in the face. Since the encounter with the dragon does not occur simultaneously with the moment of grace, as it does in "A Good Man Is Hard to Find" and "Greenleaf," there is more time for the purgatorial process within Mrs. Turpin to be shown as "Revelation" gradually changes from a comedy of rural manners into a rural Judgment Day.

Through her conversation with the others in the waiting room and the direct transcription of her thoughts, Mrs. Turpin is shown to be not only of enormous size but also of enormous complacency. Her self-satisfaction includes all aspects of her existence, from not being born black or "white-trashy" (like those in the waiting room who look "as if they would sit there until Doomsday if nobody called and told them to get up" [496]), to the cleanliness of the hogs in the "pig parlor" on her and her husband's prosperous farm. The book strikes her just after she has feelingly announced: "If it's one thing I am, it's grateful. When I think who all I could have been besides myself and what all I got, a little of everything, and a good disposition besides, I just feel like shouting 'Thank you, Jesus, for making everything the way it is! . . . Oh thank you, Jesus, Jesus, thank you!'" As her attacker is being sedated, they gaze at each other: "There was no doubt in her mind that the girl did know her in some intense and personal way, beyond time and place and condition. 'What you got to say to me?' she asked hoarsely and held her breath, waiting, as for a revelation. The girl raised her head. Her gaze locked with Mrs Turpin's. 'Go back to hell where you came from, you old wart hog,' she whispered" (499–500).

By the time she returns to her farm, it has become clear to Mrs. Turpin that her experience in the doctor's office has a special significance. "She had been singled out for the message, though there was trash in the room to whom it might justly have been applied. The full force of this fact struck her only now. . . . She was looking straight up as if there were some unintelligible handwriting on the ceiling" (502–3). This and other *as if* constructions raise a key critical consideration—marriage ring or toggle key? —and heighten the critical reader's expectation of the story's climax, which will presumably be the revelation named in the title. Mrs. Turpin goes to clean out the pig parlor as the sun is beginning to set. She glowers down at her hogs and remembers what the young woman had told her. "What did you send me a message like that for?" she says in a low, fierce voice: "How am I a hog and me both? How am I saved from hell too?" As the deepening light takes on a "mysterious hue" and the color of everything burns for a moment "with a transparent intensity," the revelation that concludes the story comes (506–7). At she lifts her head "a visionary light settle[s] in her eyes," and Mrs. Turpin sees "a vast swinging bridge extending upward from the earth through a field of living fire. Upon it a vast hoard of souls were rumbling toward heaven": companies of white trash, clean for the first time, "bands of black niggers in white robes," freaks, and lunatics; "And bringing up the end of the procession was a tribe of people whom she recognized at once as those who, like herself and Claud, had always had a little of everything and the God-given wit to use it right. She leaned forward to observe them closer. They were marching behind the others with great dignity, accountable as they had always been for good order and common sense and respectable behavior. They alone were [singing] on key. Yet she could see by their shocked and altered faces that even their virtues were being burned away" (508).

How should this revelation be described? What is its source and provenance? To borrow the terms of Wordsworth's "Resolution and Independence," is the vision a "peculiar grace, / A leading from above, a something given"; or is it rather "by [her] own powers" that Mrs. Turpin is "deified" in the sense of raised up to a vision of last things during an expansion-of-consciousness experience? One need not agree with a comment in a letter of O'Connor's that seems to suggest that the vision was a bestowal—"She gets the vision. Wouldn't have been any point in that story if she hadn't. . . . She's a country female Jacob. And that vision is purgatorial" (HB, 577). Moreover, the two as if figures that precede the revelation do not overwrite but are equivocal in implication: "she bent her head slowly and gazed, as if through the very heart of mystery, down into the pig parlor at the hogs . . . as if she were absorbing some abysmal life-giving knowledge." The answer, then, is that the source of the vision is indeterminate in a way that suggests the interpenetration of mystery and manners.

There is also a third explanation of the vision's source and provenance: it comes from the pen of Flannery O'Connor, an uncommonly gifted writer of well-made short stories, and it neatly brings together in reverse order of precedence the human types that Mrs. Turpin had earlier observed on her farm and in the waiting room, in which at one point a gospel hymn, "When I Looked Up and He Looked Down," was playing on the radio, to which Mrs. Turpin had mentally supplied the last line: "And wona these days I know I'll we-eara crown" (490). From the point of view of the well-wrought-urn tenets of the New Criticism, the concluding vision is a literary device that effectively clicks the story tightly shut—like the two signifying moments at the end of "A Temple of the Holy Ghost." While this is formally satisfying, in my view it weakens the affective and conceptual dimensions of the mystery-manners mixture in this Christian-realist short story. After all, for the vision to be ascribed to Mrs. Turpin presupposes what is hardly credible psychologically: her unconscious reconceptualization and subsequent panoramic visualization of her place in the economy of salvation. And for a divine origin to be ascribed to the vision presupposes not that God writes straight with crooked lines (as the Portuguese proverb has it), but rather that God inscribes his messages with caricatural clarity rather than mysteriously. If neither alternative is credible, then an equivocal reading of the ending can be only notionally satisfying for a reader such as myself: one delights in the artistry, but is not deeply engaged.

5

One feature of the ending of "Revelation" is not disputable: it is a rare instance in O'Connor's canon of the comparatively genial and encompassing end of her fictional spectrum of human participation in the divine—the Broad Church end, so to speak, rather than the Fundamentalist. In two other stories, "The River" and "Parker's Back," the vision is far from genial. Both are rooted in Fundamentalist Christian religious experience and are also among her most compelling and engaging representations of religious mystery.

"The River" begins with a neglected five-year-old only child being picked up in the early morning from the apartment of his hungover parents by the woman engaged to care for him for the day. The little boy seems "mute and patient, like an old sheep waiting to be let out." Mrs. Connin tells him they are "going to the river to a healing" at which the Reverend Bevel Summers will preach. She then asks the boy his first name: "His name was Harry Ashfield and he had never thought at any time before of changing it. 'Bevel,' he said" (157–59). This is the first of a number of arresting external notations that give a sense of the inner life of the sheeplike five-year-old. The outside point of view is for the most part maintained throughout the story and is the narratorial key to the sense of religious mystery that the story generates. In "Parker's Back," as we shall see, temporal and psychological omniscience are the means through which the inner life of the central character is presented and the religious plane introduced. As a result, that story is richer in cognitive import than "The River," in which the principal mode of reader engagement is affective receptivity.

Harry/Bevel and Mrs. Connin first stop at her house. When he asks who is the man in the sheet in the picture over her bed, she tells him it is Jesus, who made him. Then her sons bring Harry/Bevel out to the hog pen and cruelly tell him he can see the pigs if he lifts a bottom board and looks in. The city boy does so, expecting to see the "small fat pink animals with curly tails and round grinning faces and bow ties" that he knows from books. Instead, he finds himself confronted by a face "gray, wet and sour" (161–62). The result is a subjectively terrifying experience. The pig pushes into his face, escapes from the pen, knocks him down, snorts over him, and chases the screaming boy across a field. Back in the house, Harry/Bevel finds a book entitled "The Life of Jesus Christ for Readers under Twelve" and is struck by a picture of Jesus driving a crowd of real-looking pigs out of a man. He furtively takes the book with him to the river, where the young preacher is standing out in the current. He lifts his arms and shouts to those gathered: "There ain't but one river and that's the River of Life, made out of Jesus' Blood." Hearing that a child with the same name as his is among them and is not baptized, the preacher asks that the boy be handed out to him. Harry/Bevel has "a sudden feeling that this was not a joke. Where he lived everything was a joke" (165, 167).

> "If I Baptize you," the preacher said, "you'll be able to go to the King-dom of Christ. You'll be washed in the river of suffering, son, and you'll go by the deep river of life. Do you want that?" "Yes," the child said, and thought, I won't go back to the apartment then, I'll go under the river. "You won't be the same again," the preacher said. "You'll count." (168)

Back at the apartment, as his mother puts the boy to bed that night, it seems "as if he were under the river and she on top of it." His last words before sleep are "He said I'm not the same now. . . . I count." The next morning, the boy gets up early. After emptying two full ashtrays onto the rug and rubbing in the contents, he begins to think about the river: "Very slowly, his expression changed as if he were gradually seeing appear what he didn't know he'd been looking for. Then all of a sudden he knew what he wanted to do." Harry/Bevel makes his way to the river alone intending "not to fool with preachers anymore but to Baptize himself and keep on going this time until he found the Kingdom of Christ in the river." He is noticed by Mr. Paradise, a huge, porcine old man with a cancerous purple bulge over his ear, who had attended the previous day's healing to show once again that he had not been healed. He follows the boy, having taken from the candy shelf of his store "a peppermint stick, a foot long and two inches thick." The implication is that Mr. Paradise is a sexual predator and that the phallic candy stick is bait. As the boy wades out to immerse himself in the river he hears a shout and turns to see "something like a giant pig bounding after him." Then "the waiting current caught him like a long gentle hand and pulled him swiftly forward and down" to his death (170–74).

Weinstein has well described what happens during "The River" as an "eerie synchronization. . . . Those fatigued words 'baptism' and 'purifica-tion' move from the linguistic to the phenomenal in this story [and] re-ceive an astounding fullness of meaning"; details are shown "to be echoing and double" (1993, 113). On the one hand, all the events in this gruesome and compelling story are psychologically explicable in terms of the subjective experience of a five-year-old boy who is drawn toward Christ and his saving message because this figure seems the antithesis of the minatory fallen world of parents, jokes, ashes, and pigs. He does not distinguish between the literal and symbolic aspects of the saving waters of baptism and tragically drowns. But while the religious mystery in the story can be explained in this way, it cannot be explained away. It is rather the case that the Christian topoi of being born again in the spirit through baptism and of Christ's goodness and love triumphing over the evil symbolized by the pigs and incarnated in a piglike anti-Christ (the ironically named Mr. Paradise) have been made to resonate powerfully within the conventions of a realist short story.

The other story is "Parker's Back." Its opening poses a question for both the title character and the reader: what is the hold that Parker's wife has over her husband? She is "plain, plain. The skin on her face was thin drawn as tight as the skin of an onion and her eyes were gray and sharp like the points of two icepicks." She is also a fanatical Fundamentalist, the daughter of a Gospel preacher. She disapproves of automobiles and does not "smoke or dip, drink whiskey, use bad language or paint her face." Parker sometimes supposes that Sarah Ruth has married him because she means to save him. What he cannot understand is why he stays with her. It is "as if she had him conjured. He was puzzled and ashamed of himself" (511).

Sarah Ruth also disapproves of the tattoos that cover all parts of Parker's body except his back. In the next section of the story, the omniscient narrator retrospectively explains how and why Parker came to acquire them. At a fair when he was fourteen, he had seen a man on a platform tattooed from head to foot and flexing his muscles "so that the arabesque of men and beasts and flowers on his skin appeared to have a subtle motion of its own." The effect is to evoke in Parker for the first time in his life "the least motion of wonder" and a slight sense of the out-of-the-ordinary: "It was as if a blind boy had been turned so gently in a different direction that he did not know his destination had been changed." From that time he began to acquire tattoos. After one is etched he is at first pleased but inevitably becomes dissatisfied. The effect is not that of "one intricate arabesque of colors but of something haphazard and botched. A huge dissatisfaction would come over him and he would go off and find another tattooist and have another space filled up" (513–14).

Concerning the origin of Parker's obsession with tattoos, the narrator also reports: "Until he saw the man at the fair, it did not enter his head that there was anything out of the ordinary about the fact that he existed. Even then it did not enter his head, but a peculiar unease settled in him" (513). For André Bleikasten, this is an invitation to read the origin of Parker's obsession with tattoos "less spiritually and more psychologically, as the beginning of an 'identity crisis,' a period of psychic disturbance" in which "what seems to be at stake . . . is above all his *body*." Parker is awakened to "the exorbitant demands of narcissism"; his "systematic adornment of his skin" illustrates his narcissistic fantasies; and turning his body "into a living fetish" attests to his desire for "sexual daring, sexual potency, and unrestrained sexual gratification." This is a strong reading; but it does not explain Parker's attraction to Sarah Ruth, who, Bleikasten admits, "in all conceivable respects is his very opposite." Given his antipathy to the religious dimensions of O'Connor's stories, all Bleikasten can offer is a secular thematic gloss: Sarah Ruth represents "the radical otherness of the Law" and brings Parker to acknowledge "the accepted standards of a cultural order" (1982, 11–13).

The key to a more satisfying explanation of Sarah Ruth's presence in "Parker's Back," that better attests to the story's densely woven texture, is found in the connection between Parker's chronically dissatisfied fascination with tattoos and his dissatisfied cleaving to his ugly wife. Background information concerning the latter is supplied by a retrospective account of their courtship that parallels the retrospective account of the origin of Parker's fascination with tattoos. At one point during their first acquaintance, Sarah Ruth had asked him his full name, and when told it was "O. E. Parker" had asked what the initials stood for. With great reluctance he revealed that he was named Obadiah Elihue. Presumably because they are Old Testament names, her face brightens when she hears the first, "as if the name came as a sign to her," and then repeats both names "in a reverent voice." At this point, Parker begins to sense a connection between his feeling for his wife and his tattoos: "A dim, half-formed inspiration began to work in his mind. He visualized having a tattoo put [on his back] that Sarah Ruth would not be able to resist—a religious subject" (517–19).

A bizarre accident involving a burning tree is perceived by Parker as a liminal moment in his life and prompts him to leave immediately for the city to acquire this final tattoo. Looking through a book of religious illustrations, he is struck by "the haloed head of a flat stern Byzantine Christ with all-demanding eyes. He sat there trembling; his heart began slowly to beat again as if he were being brought to life by a subtle power. . . . He felt as though, under their gaze, he was as transparent as the wings of a fly." When he returns home after two days with this full-size image tattooed on his back, his wife refuses to let him in until he identifies himself not as

O. E. but as Obadiah Elihue. As he does so, he feels light from the sky "pouring through him, turning his spider soul into a perfect arabesque of colors, a garden and trees and birds and beasts" (522–24, 528).

This is the climactic moment of the story, in which the relationship between Parker's tattoos and his ugly wife is revealed. All his life without realizing it, Parker had been Christ-haunted—this is why earlier in the story he had been described as feeling as if someone were after him and as "turning around abruptly as if someone were trailing him" (519–20). He has finally come into his religious birthright—signified by the Old Testament names given him by his Methodist mother. Parker's attraction to the arabesque shimmer of tattoos is explained as a profane slaking of a thirst for the sacred, just as the "icepick eyes" of Sarah Ruth are a version of the powerful life-giving eyes of the Byzantine Christ. More generally, Sarah Ruth's hold over her husband is explained by the fact that she seems to him a vessel of the godliness he has been unconsciously yearning for.[3]

The story, however, does not end with the haphazard elements of Parker's being finally harmonized. There follows an extraordinary final page which bespeaks the fact that "Parker's Back" is as much a comic story as a conversion story, as much a "parable-like tall tale in the tradition of frontier and southern country humor" (Stephens 1973, 16) as a prose-fiction version of Francis Thompson's "The Hound of Heaven," and as much a story about Fundamentalist manners as about supernatural mystery. Sarah Ruth comes outside, sees the tattooed Christ on her husband's back, and is horrified. For her, visual images of Christ are a great sin. "I can put up with lies and vanity but I don't want no idolator in this house," she screams at him, before grabbing a broom and thrashing him with it, just as she had done at their first meeting because of his taking the name of the Lord in vain. Before she stops, large welts have formed on the face of the Christ tattoo. Back in the house alone, she looks out the window toward the pecan tree and—in the story's final lines—"her eyes hardened still more. There he was—who called himself Obadiah Elihue—leaning against the tree, crying like a baby" (529–30). The simile as readily suggests exasperated exhaustion as it does rebirth. Thus, at the end of the story, the question of

---

3. O'Connor's habitual figural embellishments also alert the reader to the religious plane of the story. Sarah Ruth is compared to "a giant hawk-eyed angel wielding a hoary weapon"; calm descends "as if the long barnlike room were the ship from which Jonah had been cast into the sea" (527); and, of course, the burning tree alludes to the angel of the Lord appearing to Moses out of a burning bush in Exodus 3:2.

whether Parker has been the recipient of a saving supernatural grace remains problematic.

6

For one of her secular critics, "when one takes the stories altogether, the relentlessly narrow O'Connor view of human affairs tends to weigh on the reader much more heavily, to come much closer—than any one story taken separately—to a falsification of human experience as most of us know it" (Stephens 1973, 145). Prima facie, one can see the point of this observation. O'Connor herself, for example, recognized that sexual love was not within her scope as a creative writer and was acutely aware of the seriousness of the omission. "You are . . . very right about the lacking category [love and sexuality]," she tells a correspondent, "which reminds me that Chekhov said 'he-and-she is the machine that makes fiction work,' or something like that. . . . My inability to handle it so far in fiction may be purely personal, as my upbringing has smacked a little of Jansenism even if my convictions do not. But there is also the fact that being for me the center of life and most holy, I should keep my hands off it until I feel that what I can do with it will be right, which is to say, given" (*HB*, 117). But as a *critical* observation about O'Connor's fiction, the suggestion that she falsified "human experience as most of us know it" is factitious. It is not the breadth of human experience that is the crucial determinant of the status of a writer's short stories, but rather what the writer does creatively with his/her given. Raymond Carver, for example, wrote about little other than the vicissitudes of sexual love. Is it a falsification of their creative work that he and O'Connor leave out much of human experience as most of us know it? Not if the task of the short-story writer is to invest the glimpse that is the story with as much power as he/she can, which for a realist writer means writing stories that are necessarily rooted in one's felt experience of life. It is to a consideration of the fictional distillation of Carver's experience of life that I now turn.

1

Raymond Carver's career as a short-story writer began with an unmistakable swerve away from Hemingway that took the form of a rewriting of "Big Two-Hearted River." The ironically titled "Pastoral," published in 1963, when Carver was in his midtwenties, was slightly revised and republished as "The Cabin" in 1986 (the version I cite). The story narrates the solitary return of a Mr. Harrold to a river he has fished in the past and where he rehearses once again the known and loved rituals of fishing. As Nick Adams does, he is careful to defer his pleasures, and when he first casts his line, like Nick he feels "some of the old excitement coming back." Later, resting on the river bank, "he wasn't going to hurry anything," just as Nick "did not want to rush his sensations any" (152).

Such similarities make the differences between the stories all the more telling. G. P. Lainsbury scarcely exaggerates in noting that "Everything about Mr. Harrold's return to this place is a corrupted version of Nick Adams's experience" (2004, 37). Nick backpacks his gear a considerable distance on a hot summer day to the place where he makes a "good camp" for himself; Carver's protagonist drives up in the snow to a lodge identified by a flickering neon sign, where he has booked one of the "Deluxe Cabins." Shlock tourist items are for sale at the lodge, and an outbuilding has been vandalized by local adolescents, children of workers at a nearby construction camp. Nick's neck and back hurt from carrying his pack; he rests them during a nap in the shade of pine trees and wakes refreshed. Mr. Harrold's neck and back are stiff from his car drive; his indoor nap is much longer than he intended, and when he wakes he is angry with himself for missing the chance to fish that afternoon. When he does get to the cold river the next morning, his experience is traumatic. At the end of Hemingway's story, Nick decides to put off for another day fishing in the minatory swamp. But Mr. Harrold cannot defer his encounter first with a wounded female deer with mucus hanging from its nostrils and a broken leg dangling behind, and then with the adolescents from the construction camp who shot her. They appear on the bank while Harrold is wading defenseless in the stream, taunt him, make obscene gestures, point a rifle at his genitals, and throw rocks at him.

Lainsbury argues that "The Cabin" is concerned with the possibility of the existence in late-twentieth-century America of "something heroic"—a too-explicit phrase from the last paragraph of the story's first version. This critic certainly has a point—as the contrast between the debased deer hunt and the Indian buffalo hunt depicted in a Frederic Remington reproduction on a wall in the lodge suggests. But Carver's story is more concerned with the continuity between the central character's younger self and his troubled adult self, and subcutaneously with the married state (also a concern of Hemingway's "Now I Lay Me," a story closely linked to "Big Two-Hearted River"). In each case, the implications are negative. An inserted memory is telling. Mr. Harrold recalls going as a adolescent to fish in a remote area. Hiking in by himself, carrying his rod "tucked up under his arm like a lance . . . he would imagine himself waiting for his opponent to ride out of the trees on a horse." He also remembers in Hemingway-like cadences the way it was perceptually: "The sun and the sky came back to him now, and the lake with the lean-to. The water was so clear and green you could see fifteen or twenty feet down to where it shelved off into deeper water" (151). Carver's protagonist does not reflect on the then-now difference; but for the reader aware of the intertextual dynamics between this story and the Nick Adams sequence it is hard not to remember Nick's lament in "Fathers and Sons": "Long time ago good. Now no good" (498). Mr. Harrold also remembers that in the past he often used to come to fish the river with his wife. Now he comes alone—but there are reminders that she is on his mind, as when he notices a young couple and "the way the man held the woman's arm as they went down the steps" or remembers her not liking the Chinese landscapes he had admired during a museum visit. And it is telling that when he tries not to think about the wounded deer, he immediately thinks: "Frances would be up now, doing things around the house. He didn't want to think about Frances, either" (146, 153). It is a striking association—wounded deer / wounded relationship. Nick goes back to his river to assuage a psychological wound; Mr. Harrold seems to return to his river for the same reason; but it is intimated that the cause of his wound is marriage-related rather than war-related.

After the boys leave, Mr. Harrold flees the river, abandoning in his haste his fishing rod (metonymically suggestive of the chivalric daydreams of his younger self and his relationship to the natural world; metaphorically suggestive of his virility). Recovering his composure at the cabin, he first thinks of the river he has left behind. Then (in the story's closing words), "He began to think of home, of getting back there before dark" (156). But one is given no reason to think that this domestic space will prove any warmer and less heart-stopping than the cold water of the river.

2

The Hemingway career trajectory—from America to Europe, Africa, and the Gulf Stream—was very different from Carver's. His obscure track led to small cities and suburbs in lower-middle-class America among the working poor he writes about—undereducated whites without marketable skills leading dreary, unfulfilled lives in tacky surroundings. The almost-never-realized hopes of his characters are simple. The title character of "The Student's Wife" tells her husband: "I'd like to stop moving around every year, or every other year. Most of all . . . I'd like us both just to live a good honest life without having to worry about money and bills and things like that"; and the male protagonist of "Menudo" wishes "I could be like everybody else in this neighborhood—your basic, normal, unaccomplished person—and go up to my bedroom, and lie down, and sleep" (39–40, 461). Unsurprisingly, in Carver's stories there are many failed or failing relationships; and much chain-smoking and alcoholism.

Despite the differences, Hemingway remained a crucial point of reference for Carver in terms of both technique and stance. Concerning the former, as has often been noted, the stories of both are written in what Carver calls "common language, the language of normal discourse, the language we speak to each other in" (*Call,* 104). In both, the unadorned prose complements the compression of detail, slightness of incident, and the omission of explanation that requires readers to fill in the gaps—the emotions, understandings, or misunderstandings that lie beneath the surface of the narrative. The similarities are perhaps seen most clearly in Carver's one-scene stories depicting crisis points in deteriorating relationships. These recall Hemingway stories such as "Cat in the Rain," "The Sea Change," and his minimalist masterpiece, "Hills Like White Elephants." Indeed, at one point in the last story the female character asks the male, "Would you

please please please please please please please stop talking?" (277), a line
that is echoed in the title of Carver's story "Will You Please Be Quiet,
Please?"[1]

An example of continuities in stance is Carver's adaptation of Hemingway's fatalistic code. This was first called attention to by Eugene Goodheart,
who noted that "like Hemingway's characters, Carver's characters possess a
code (there is even the code of the alcoholic) which dictates their behavior. There is a right way and a wrong way to be despairing, or ineffectual,
or lost" (1987, 164). As a young man, Carver learned "that I had to bend or
else break. And I also learned that it is possible to bend and break at the
same time" (*Call,* 102). In this situation, the most one can hope to achieve
is a certain stoicism in defeat and an unillusioned acceptance of the in-
evitable. This is the point in the exchange between husband and wife in
"Chef's House" when it is becoming clear to both that he is going to return
to his alcoholic ways. She narrates:

> Then I said something. I said, Suppose, just suppose, nothing had ever
> happened. Suppose this was for the first time. Just suppose. It doesn't hurt
> to suppose. Say none of the other had ever happened. You know what I
> mean? Then what? I said.
>
> Wes fixed his eyes on me. He said, Then I suppose we'd have to be
> somebody else if that was the case. Somebody we're not. I don't have
> that kind of supposing left in me. We were born who we are. Don't you
> see what I'm saying?
>
> I said I hadn't thrown away a good thing and come six hundred miles
> to hear him talk like this.
>
> He said, I'm sorry, but I can't talk like somebody I'm not. I'm not
> somebody else. If I was somebody else, I sure as hell wouldn't be here. If
> I was somebody else, I wouldn't be me. But I'm who I am. Don't you see?
> (301–2)

Stories informed by this bleak vision present challenges for commentators. It is a comparatively simple critical task to describe the uplifting

1. On several occasions Carver expressed his dislike of being called a "'minimalist' writer. . . . There's something about 'minimalist' that smacks of smallness of
vision and execution that I don't like" (Conv, 44). But he would hardly have disagreed with the "many scholars [who] believe that minimalism, as it is called, is not
so much a break with modernism as it is a carryover from the Hemingway-type story
with its sparseness of detail and objective stance" (Iftekharrudin 2003, xi). On the
minimalist short story and its continuities with earlier realist short fiction, see Cynthia J. Hallett.

endings of a very few Carver stories in ways that at the same time valorize the story. An example is Carver's best-known story, "Cathedral," which he described as "more affirmative" than earlier stories and written in a "fuller, more generous" manner (*Conv*, 125, 199). The story recounts an evening the narrator and his wife spend in their home with a houseguest—a blind man named Robert, an old friend of the wife whom she has not seen for some years. In his retelling, the husband does nothing to conceal his truculence and reluctance to welcome the guest: "This blind man . . . he was on his way to spend the night. . . . A blind man in my house was not something I looked forward to." And he reports that when he sarcastically tells his wife, "I don't have any blind friends," she replies, "You don't have *any* friends" (356, 359).

At the end of the evening, the wife is asleep on the couch while the narrator watches a television program about cathedrals and Robert listens to the commentary. When the blind man asks him to describe a cathedral, the narrator finds it difficult to do so: "The truth is, cathedrals don't mean anything special to me. Nothing. Cathedrals. They're something to look at on late-night TV. That's all they are." Robert then suggests that they draw a cathedral together with his hands closed over the narrator's. "So I began. First I drew a box that looked like a house. It could have been the house I lived in. Then I put a roof on it. At either end of the roof I drew spires. Crazy. 'Swell,' he said. 'Terrific.'" The narrator keeps on drawing, adding windows, flying buttresses, doors, and people. When he finishes, the story ends:

> So we kept on with it. His fingers rode my fingers as my hand went over the paper. It was like nothing else in my life up to now.
> Then he said, "I think that's it. I think you got it," he said. "Take a look, What do you think?"
> But I had my eyes closed. I thought I'd keep them that way for a little longer. I thought it was something I ought to do.
> "Well," he said, "Are you looking?"
> My eyes were still closed. I was in my house. I knew that. But I didn't feel I was inside anything.
> "It's really something," I said. (372–75)

While less affirmative than some commentators have taken it to be, the ending unquestionably conveys an exhilarating sense of gain and liberation: "something" has replaced "nothing" in the narrator's being, and the costive house of quotidian life in which he had been immured has become a large airy enclosure. His cathedral-drawing with the blind man does for the narrator what Carver claims the finest stories do for readers: move "our hearts or our intellects . . . off the peg just a little from where they were before" (*Call*, 201–2). Of course, how long the narrator will remain in this expansive state of being is another matter—one that "Cathedral" does not concern itself with.

In contrast, most of Carver's stories do no more than powerfully communicate a sense of the quiet desperation of their characters' lives. "Where I'm Calling From" is an example. The story's literal setting is a detox house with a telephone; its figurative location is *de profundis*—the rock bottom that the first-person narrator has reached. A literal depth is described when the narrator recounts the background of another recovering alcoholic in the house who at the age of twelve had had the terrifying experience of falling into a dry well, hollering for help, and waiting. But while he waited, "nothing fell on him and nothing closed off that little circle of blue" (281). This could be taken to suggest the possibility of a similar rise from the depths for the narrator. But the opposite is suggested by his later remembering a story by Jack London, who is on his mind because the manager of the drying-out facility had told him that the American writer "used to have a big place on the other side of this valley. . . . But alcohol killed him. Let that be a lesson to you. He was a better man than any of us. But he couldn't handle the stuff, either" (288). The remembered story is "To Build a Fire," at the end of which the central character freezes to death in the Yukon snows after doing the pitifully little that he can to avoid this fate. Carver's story ends with the narrator thinking about using the change in his pocket to call either his estranged wife or his estranged girlfriend. As at the end of a number of Hemingway's stories, the point is that it is important for a person to have something, no matter what, to look forward to because it helps to keep at bay the recognition that there may in fact be nothing positive in one's future. In this way, "Where I'm Calling From" stops rather than ends, suggesting neither that the narrator will be rescued from his well nor that he will perish in the cold. As Carver notes of the endings of his stories, "It would be inappropriate, and to a degree impossible, to resolve things neatly for these people and situations I'm writing about" (*Conv*, 111).

3

Given the limitations of his subject matter, the minimalist means and the bleak vision, it might be thought that the cumulative effect of a reading of the 526 pages of Carver's *Where I'm Calling From: New and Selected Stories* would be tedium and depression. The thought seems to have occurred to

Carver, to judge by a self-reflexive passage in his late story, "Menudo." An adulterous couple is talking in a coffee shop:

> "Who reads? Do you read?" (I shook my head.) "Someone must read, I guess. You see all those books around in store windows, and there are those clubs. Somebody's reading," she said. "Who? I don't know anybody who reads."
>
> That's what she said, apropos of nothing—that is, we weren't talking about books, we were talking about our *lives*. Books had nothing to do with it.
>
> "What did Oliver say when you told him?"
>
> Then it struck me that what we were saying—the tense, watchful expressions we wore—belonged to the people on afternoon TV programs that I'd never done more than switch on and then off. (456)

The self-undermining suggestion is that if a book such as *Where I'm Calling From* has no value for the kind of characters it depicts, and if their problems and linguistic registers do not rise above the level of those found on soap operas, then there is little profit in anyone reading the book.

So provoked, I would answer by saying that it is presumptuous to assume that Carver's subject matter and presentational mode are other than the deliberate choice of an intelligent and inventive writer who would surely agree with Brian Moore that "failure is a more interesting condition than success. Success changes people; it makes them something they were not . . . whereas failure leaves you with a more intense distillation of that self you are" (qtd. Girson 1962, 20). The variety of ways in which this essence is distilled—different angles of narration, different phases of marital relationships highlighted, meaningful detail, self-reflexive elements—and the aesthetic pleasure given by the skillful amalgamation of the ingredients are central aspects of Carver's achievement as a short-story writer. And while their subject matter and presentational mode usually preclude their being rich in cognitive implication, the stories are profitable and meaningful in terms of the awareness they create in the reader. Carver could have been speaking of his own work when he observed that literature "can make us aware of some of our lacks, some things in our lives that diminish us, that have diminished us, and it can make us realize what it takes to be human, to be something larger than we really are, something better. I think literature can make us realize that our lives are not being lived to the fullest possible extent" (*Conv*, 130).

Let us consider a pair of two-character stories. "Neighbors" derives from Maupassant's "The Conservatory," in which sexual relations between a husband and wife are rejuvenated and civility between them restored by first the husband and then both of them going on moonlit nights to the conservatory at the end of their garden and silently watching through a window while their maid and her lover pleasure each other. Carver has refashioned Maupassant's worldly anecdote into an original and disturbing story of triangular or mediated desire. "Bill and Arlene Miller were a happy couple," the story begins: "But now and then they felt they alone among their circle had been passed by somehow." In particular, it seems to them that their friends and across-the-hall neighbors, Harriet and Jim Stone, "lived a fuller and brighter life" (861). The Millers promise to feed the cat and water the plants in the Stones' apartment while they are away. Also leaving the story at this time is the omniscience of the narrator, who offers inside views of his central characters only in the opening paragraph. Afterward he is strictly objective in his narration with no explanations offered and, until the story's final sentence, no figural embellishment.

On the first night of the Stones' absence, Bill goes across the hall. While the cat is feeding, he goes into the bathroom, "looked at himself in the mirror and then closed his eyes and then looked again" (87). The suggestion is that he is beginning to see another person. He then takes a container of prescription pills and slips it into his pocket. Before leaving the apartment he also takes two swigs from a bottle of expensive scotch. Back in his own apartment, he greets his wife by touching her breasts and suggesting they go to bed. He makes the same suggestion the next day as soon as they get home from work. The following day he skips works and spends it in the Stones' apartment. He lies on their bed, closes his eyes, stimulates himself, dresses in Jim's clothes, has a drink, tries on a pair of Harriet's panties and a brassiere, puts on a white checkered skirt and burgundy blouse, and then stares out the window for a long time. That evening Arlene goes to feed the cat. When she eventually returns, Bill notices white lint clinging to the back of her sweater and high color in her cheeks, which signal that she too has been sexually stirred by illicit intimacies. They begin kissing, but then she remembers that she has forgotten to feed the cat and water the plants. She also remembers to mention that she has found some pictures (presumably erotic) in a drawer, and she further remarks that "Maybe they won't come back," echoing a thought her husband has had. Holding hands, they cross the hall to the Stones' front door, at which point Arlene realizes she has left the key inside. The story ends as follows: "He tried the knob. It was locked. Then she tried the knob. It would not turn. Her lips were parted, and her breathing was hard, expectant. He opened his arms and she moved into them. 'Don't worry,' he said into her ear. 'For God's sake, don't worry.' They stayed there. They held each other. They leaned into the door as if against a wind, and braced themselves" (92–93).

The couple is hardly distraught because of the misplaced key, which the building superintendent can help them retrieve. It is rather the case that the ending registers their shock at realizing what one commentator calls "the enormity of their libidinal investment in what has amounted to a virtual transformation of their identities" (Cornwell 2005, 351) but what I would describe as the degrading nature of their desires and the futility of their attempt to escape their identities. The gravity of their situation is registered by the conspicuous *as if* figuration (as surprising to find in a Carver story as it is predictable to find in one of O'Connor's), which recalls the carnal sinners blown about by winds of lust in the fifth canto of Dante's *Inferno*. In the final sentence, Bill and Arlene Miller brace themselves for reentry into their normal lives. A voyeuristic experience that is wholly positive in Maupassant's story functions in Carver's as an ephemeral titillation that leaves behind an intensified sense of diminished existence.

The other story, "Intimacy," opens abruptly in the present tense with the male narrator explaining that since he is out west anyway he decides to pay a visit to his ex-wife, whom he has not seen in four years. It ends with his leaving her home after a "real time" visit. The principal voice in the story is that of the wife, who is full of bitter recrimination: "Can you imagine it?" she exclaims, "We were so *intimate* once upon a time. I can't believe it now" (446). But her discourse is framed within the consciousness of the male narrator as focalizer, and the reader is thus given a indirect or mediated representation of her speech. The effect is to distance the reader slightly from what the characters are also at a distance from—their former intimacy, of which only the afterlife remains.

This distance also helps the reader to realize that "Intimacy" has a self-reflexive dimension. The narrator is a writer, and the ex-wife has suspicions about what might have motivated his visit: "But you're a slyboots. You know why you're here. You're on a fishing expedition. You're hunting for *material*." One of her principal accusations concerns his previous fictional re-creations of their marital intimacy: "you remember the wrong things. You remember the low, shameful things . . . you held me up for display and ridicule in your so-called work." His reply is to admit that "I hold to the dark view of things. Sometimes, anyway." And when they are saying goodbye, she observes of their meeting: "Maybe it'll make a good story. . . . But I don't want to know about it if it does" (447–53). These remarks

insure that the reader's engagement with the story will include a consideration of whether the narrator-writer is parasitic, whether the story he
has written holds to the dark view of things, and whether it is "a good
story."

The turning point in "Intimacy" occurs when the narrator gets down on
his knees: "What am I doing on the floor? I wish I could say. But I know
it's where I ought to be, and I'm there on my knees holding on to the hem
of her dress." This gesture effects a change in the wife, leading her to say
that if he will get up and go she will say something. "She says, I forgive
you." She even seems to give him a sort of benediction when she says: "You
just tell it like you have to, I guess, and forget the rest" (450–52). But this
statement can be read two ways—read straight, she is encouraging him to
tell it like it is and be unconcerned with anything else. Read ironically, the
meaning is: all you do is express your view of things with no consideration
for others. This invigorating ambiguity is complemented at the story's end
by two striking details that are similarly equivocal in their signification.
As the narrator walks out the door, "I look outside, and Jesus, there's this
white moon hanging in the morning sky. I can't think when I've ever seen
anything so remarkable." And as he moves off down the sidewalk, he
notices that "There are these leaves everywhere, even in the gutters. Piles
of leaves wherever I look. I can't take a step without putting my shoe into
leaves. Somebody ought to make an effort here. Somebody ought to get a
rake and take care of this" (452–53).

Both details figure the reduction to residue of the couple's former intimacy; the moon is "lovely in waning but lustreless" like the celestial body
in Gerard Manley Hopkins's poem "Moonrise"; and the falling and gather-
ing up of leaves are natural-cycle correlatives for loss and the persistence of
memory images. As such, these figures might be said to help the story to
end on a softly autumnal note. But both figures are also conventional and
hackneyed: the association of the moon with romantic love is a cliché; and
when Dante Rossetti's speaker in "Autumn Song" asks, "Knowest thou not
at the fall of a leaf / How the soul feels like a dried sheaf?," the answer is
that everyone knows this. Moreover, the staleness of both figures reminds
the reader that falling on one's knees and touching a garment's hem is
hardly a fresh posture of contrition. When read in the context of the self-
reflexive dimension of "Intimacy," these figures suggest not the soft view,
but the dark view: the emotional and creative exhaustion of the writer
finally out of material and no longer able to write a good story. But the narrator is not the author of "Intimacy," which is an excellent story in which
Carver's dark view of things is freshly embodied.

4

Marital relationships in a certain part of the American social spectrum is Carver's principal topos or—to use an idiom closer to that of his characters —his bread-and-butter subject. Among the more sustained and resonant handlings of the material are three longer stories—"What's in Alaska?" "What We Talk about When We Talk about Love," and "Feathers"—that when clustered make up a little trilogy on the subject of married love and its vicissitudes in late-twentieth-century America. All describe in detail a social occasion in a home involving two couples; and all offer a dark view of things. But each story is different from the others in mode of presentation, cast of characters, and affective impact. The first employs a strictly objective third-person narrator. It opens with Jack buying a new pair of shoes on his way home from work. When he arrives at their apartment, the first thing his wife, Mary, tells him is that she does not like the color of the shoes, which puts him slightly out of sorts for the rest of the evening ("on a little bummer" is her expression for it [73]). Before they leave for an evening out, Mary also tells him she has had a job interview and may well be offered a position in Alaska. At Carl and Helen's, the foursome get stoned on marijuana with the help of the host's new water pipe. They also partake of popsicles, M&Ms, potato chips, corn chips, onion-flavored snack crackers, U-No bars, and cream soda. Much of the account of the evening consists of verbatim-seeming transcriptions of the couples' banal, frequently inane, and increasingly off-the-beat conversational exchanges:

"What about some cream soda?" Carl said.
Mary and Helen laughed.
"What about it?" Mary said.
"Well, I thought we were going to have a glass," Carl said. He looked at Mary and grinned
Mary and Helen laughed.
"What's funny?" Carl said. He looked at Helen and then at Mary. He shook his head. "I don't know about you guys," he said.
"We might go to Alaska," Jack said.
"Alaska?" Carl said. "What's in Alaska? What would you do up there?"
"I wish we could go someplace," Helen said.
"What's wrong with here?" Carl said. "What would you guys do in Alaska? I'm serious. I'd like to know."
Jack put a potato chip in his mouth and sipped his cream soda. "I don't know. What did you say?"

> After a while Carl said, "What's in Alaska?"
> "I don't know," Jack said. "Ask Mary. Mary knows. Mary, what am
> I going to do up there? Maybe I'll grow those giant cabbages you read
> about."
> "Or pumpkins," Helen said. "Grow pumpkins."
> "You'd clean up," Carl said. "Ship the pumpkins down here for
> Halloween. I'll be your distributor." (75–76)

Several incidents punctuate the evening's verbal vacuity. In one, Jack spills cream soda on his new shoes and pronounces them ruined. In another, watching Mary and Carl in the kitchen, Jack notices that she puts her arms around his waist. This is one of several fleeting notations that suggest the possibility of an illicit intimacy between the two.[2] The principal incident involves Carl and Helen's cat, Cindy. It enters with a mouse in its mouth, settles under the coffee table, and holds the mouse in its paws, licking it slowly from head to tail before ingesting it. On the way home, Mary tells Jack that "I want to be fucked, talked to, diverted. Divert me, Jack. I need to be diverted tonight" (83–84). But in their bedroom she asks for a drink, uses a sip of the beer to swallow the pill she had almost forgotten to take (presumably for birth control), repeats the story's title phrase, and falls asleep. While she snores next to him, Jack stares into the darkness of the hall. He thinks he sees something with small eyes staring at him and picks up one of his now-unwanted new shoes to throw. He is waiting tensely for the something to make a noise when the story ends.

In reflecting on the implications of the representation of this joyless evening, one is helped by two glosses (so to speak) supplied by the implied author. One is the flagrant signifier of the cat carrying the dead mouse. It is a prolepsis, and perhaps the subjective cause, of the obscure menace Jack feels at the end of the story from the small-eyed something in the hall. It

2. It is true that Carver assured an interviewer that in the story, "There's an affair going on between the husband's friend and his wife" (Conv, 163). But this retrospective comment suggests that the author had lost his feel for the story. The comment has unfortunately encouraged some commentators, such as Arthur F. Bethea in the second chapter of his *Technique and Sensibility in the Fiction and Poetry of Raymond Carver* (New York: Routledge, 2001), to over-read, manipulating details until an adulterous affair is substantiated to their satisfaction and thus destroying the effect of Carver's minimalist presentation. The fleeting glimpses subliminally suggest the possibility of a adulterous relationship; since they are not substantiated they further suggest that the putative affair is as random and mindless as the activities that are described in the story.

is also a demeaning comment on the couples who have spent the evening licking popsicles and sucking on a water pipe; and in its sexual connotations a demeaning suggestion of the quality of the physical intimacy that perhaps exists between Mary and Carl. The other gloss, the story's title, has a similar dual implication. Alaska comes up for a second time in the story when Carl asks with a certain urgency: "'What *about* Alaska, you guys?' 'There's nothing in Alaska,' Jack said. 'He's on a bummer,' Mary said. 'What'll you guys *do* in Alaska?' Carl said. 'There's nothing to do in Alaska,' Jack said. He put his feet under the coffee table. Then he moved them out under the light once more. 'Who wants a new pair of shoes?' Jack said" (80).

The characters do not know what is in Alaska—it cannot be located by their experiential compass and is beyond the limit of their expectations and imaginations. For them there is only an emptiness up there that mirrors the emptiness of their own lives as epitomized by Mary's random sexual urges and Jack's preoccupation with his cheap new shoes. At some rudimentary level, however, the idea of Alaska as the minatory obverse of their present existence does seem to affect them, as the staring eyes in the dark hall affect Jack. But the reader apprehends this much more clearly than the characters do, and it is the reader's awareness that is enlarged, not theirs.

In "What We Talk about When We Talk about Love," the economic and cultural level of the two couples is higher: we are given a foursome drinking gin with tonic around the kitchen table in a medical doctor's home. The time of day is special: "The afternoon sun was like a presence in this room, the spacious light of ease and generosity. We could have been anywhere, somewhere enchanted. We raised our glasses again [in a toast to love] and grinned at each other like children who had agreed on something forbidden" (176). What they have agreed to, or have gotten themselves into, is a discussion not of what is in Alaska, but of the nature of love. One couple, the first-person narrator, Nick, and his partner, Laura, are in the early days of their relationship: they enjoy each other's company and each other's touch, say little, and according to their host, glow with love.

Mel, the loquacious host, is a cardiologist and former Roman Catholic seminarian. He is also insecure, overbearing, opinionated, and, according to his wife, always has love on his mind. The wife is Terri, whose first husband, she recounts, had loved her so much he tried to kill her and after she left him drank rat poison before fatally shooting himself in the mouth. Mel insists that "that's not love. . . . If you call that love, you can have it" and calls Terri "a romantic . . . of the kick-me-so-I'll-know-you-love-me school." He tries to explain his own view discursively through a distinction between "physical love" or "carnal love" as opposed to "sentimental love . . . love of the other person's being, his or her essence, as it were . . . the day-to-day caring about the other person." This is his version of the familiar distinction between romantic love based on sexual attraction and companionate love. To drive home his views, he insists on telling a story to illustrate "real love," even to the point not of kicking his wife, but of ordering her to "Just shut up for once in your life" so that he can speak (171–78). His story concerns an elderly couple who survived a serious car accident. The husband had been put in a body cast and became depressed and distraught because the narrowness of its eyeholes kept him from seeing his wife: "Can you imagine? I'm telling you, the man's heart was breaking because he couldn't turn his goddamn head and *see* his goddamn wife . . . I mean, it was killing the old fart just because he couldn't *look* at the fucking woman. . . . Do you see what I'm saying?" (183).

As the expletives suggest, by this point a great deal of gin has been consumed by the couples. In Plato's *Symposium,* love as a subject for discussion is proposed by the medical doctor Eryximachus. He cautions that drunkenness is bad for people, and all the guests agree that discussion of love requires a clear head. But the heads of Carver's doctor and his interlocutors are not clear. They don't see what he is saying, and they fail to notice what the reader does—that Mel has a thing about protective body covering. Earlier in the story, he had proclaimed that if there were reincarnation, "I'd like to come back as a knight. You were pretty safe wearing all that armor . . . they couldn't get hurt very easy" (180–81). A continuing hurt of Mel's surfaces near the end of the story when he maudlinly announces he wants to call his kids. When he is reminded that his ex-wife might answer the telephone, he suddenly remembers that she is allergic to bees and says that he is "praying she'll get herself stung to death by a swarm of fucking bees." He adds that he sometimes thinks of going to her house "dressed like a beekeeper. You know, that hat that's like a helmet with the plate that comes down over your face, the big gloves, and the padded coat? I'll knock on the door and let loose a hive of bees in the house" (184–85).

The story ends when the gin runs out. What are the implications of this bibulous symposium? The views of Mel—the cardiologist who thinks he knows everything about the human heart—seem undermined by his fantasy images of himself in protective garb that are diametrically different in their implications about love from that of the old man in the protective body cast. One might further reflect that since talking about love either discursively or through telling stories (Terri's account of her first husband; Mel's account of the elderly couple) does not seem to tell one much about the subject, it is better to say little and not to generalize. As Alyokhin says in Chekhov's story "About Love": "Only one indisputable truth has ever been uttered about love, which is that 'this is a great mystery,' as it says in the Bible. . . . The explanation which seems to be right for one particular set of circumstances turns out to be wrong for a dozen others, and so the best one can do, as far as I can see, is to assess each situation on its own terms, without trying to generalize. As doctors say, you should treat each case individually" (158). "What We Talk about When We Talk about Love" shows what Chekhov's character merely states concerning the mystery of love. In the story's closing lines, the magical sunlight has gone and the narrator listens not to talk about love but to a more fundamental and menacing biological substrate of love: "I could hear my heart beating. I could hear everyone's heart. I could hear the human noise we sat there making, not one of us moving, not even when the room went dark" (185).

The third story, "Feathers," also employs a first-person narrator. But this time the *I* as experiencing self in present time is supplemented by the retrospective comments of the *I* as narrating self. His name is Jack, and he is married to Fran, "a big tall drink of water" with long blond hair. In the evening, "she'd brush her hair and we'd wish out loud for things we didn't have. . . . But one thing we didn't wish for was kids. . . . The reason we didn't have kids was that we didn't want kids. Maybe sometime, we said to each other. But right then, we were waiting" (333–34). Jack recounts the night they drove into the country for dinner at the home of Bud, a friend from work. Unlike her husband, Fran does not respond positively to the countryside—this is one of a number of details suggesting their imperfect compatibility. But they are equally struck by what greets them when they arrive at Bud's home.

> Then something as big as a vulture flapped heavily down from one of the trees and landed just in front of the car. It shook itself. It turned its long neck toward the car, raised its head and regarded us. . . .
>
> We both knew it was a peacock, sure. . . . It had fluffed itself out and looked about twice the size it'd been when it landed.
>
> "Goddamn," I said again. We stayed where we were in the front seat.
>
> The bird moved forward a little. Then it turned its head to the side and braced itself. It kept its bright, wild eye right on us. Its tail was raised, and it was like a big fan folding in and out. There was every color in the rainbow shining from that tail.
>
> "My God," said Fran quietly. She moved her hand over to my knee.
> (336)

The peacock belongs to Bud's wife, Olla, a plump little woman with her hair done up. So does the extraordinary object they notice on top of the color television in the living room—"an old plaster-of-Paris cast of the most crooked, jaggedy teeth in the world. There were no lips to the awful-looking thing, and no jaw either, just these old plaster teeth packed into something that resembled thick yellow gums" (341). The simulacra are what Olla's teeth looked like before she had braces. She explains that Bud had encouraged her to have her teeth fixed when they came together and that she keeps the cast around to remind her of how much she owes him. It is one of a number of indications that they are a happy, loving couple. As dinner is ending Olla brings to the table another indication, one that rivals the plaster teeth in ugliness: her eight-month-old baby: "It was so ugly I couldn't say anything. . . . I don't mean it was diseased or disfigured. Nothing like that. It was just ugly." The infant is restive. The reason, Olla explains, is that her peacock is used to coming into the house and "fool[ing] around with him a little before his bedtime." Its entry into the house precipitates the story's climax—an extraordinary moment as unexpected and electrifying as the climactic moment in "Cathedral." "The peacock walked quickly around the table and went for the baby. It ran its long neck across the baby's legs. It pushed its beak in under the baby's pajama top and shook its stiff head back and forth. The baby laughed and kicked its feet. Scooting onto its back, the baby worked its way over Fran's knees and down onto the floor. The peacock kept pushing against the baby, as if it was a game they were playing. Fran held the baby against her legs while the baby strained forward" (349–53).

In the story's final two pages, the narrator briefly summarizes the rest of the evening. He realizes that the occasion is special; it makes him feel good about almost everything in his life, and he makes a wish to "never forget or otherwise let go of that evening." For Fran the evening has been equally special. She sits close to Jack as they drive away and keeps her hand on his leg. And when they are home and in bed together she tells him, "Honey, fill me up with your seed" (354). For the reader of "What's in Alaska?," it is notable that she does not ask merely to be fucked—the difference being analogous to that between a peacock playing with the baby and a cat licking a dead mouse. But in the story these closing moments are not recounted in the order of their occurrence and are interspersed with after-the-fact comments by the narrating *I* concerning his and Fran's later life. One learns that his wish concerning the evening "came true. And it was bad luck for me that it did" in that they subsequently had a child but the kid had a "conniving streak" and turned out badly. And Fran got fat and cut her hair, a telling detail given the narrator's earlier mention of the fact that he fell in love with her because of her hair and would tell her that he "might stop loving her if she cut it" (354–55).

Prima facie, this after-the-story's-end information could be considered gratuitous deflationary irony reflecting Carver's temperamental predisposition to hold to "the dark view of things." But one might better suggest that at the end of the story the narrator is like the girl at the end of "Why Don't You Dance?," who senses that "there was more" to that story than she could put into words and that it is up to the reader to articulate the significance of the story's climax and ending (161). Certainly the peacock has none of the supernatural suggestiveness the peacock in O'Connor's "The Displaced Person" is given. It rather recalls the effect of the animal who appears on the highway at the climax of Elizabeth Bishop's "The Moose." The speaker of her poem re-creates a long bus ride during which she listens to passengers discussing death, illness, and the other ordinary sorrows of their lives. Suddenly the bus stops to avoid hitting a moose standing in the moonlight in the road. The passengers look out in astonishment:

> Taking her time,
> she looks the bus over,
> grand, otherworldly.
> Why, why do we feel
> (we all feel) this sweet
> sensation of joy? (173)

The sweet sensation the narrator and his wife both feel in "Feathers" has a procreative sexual dimension. But the problem with such moments of expanded consciousness is that they are exceptional and that their intensity is the antithesis of the duration that precedes and follows them. Had there been no retrospective comment on what happened to the couple after they went to bed at the end of the evening, the close of "Feathers" would have been as affirmative as that of "Cathedral." But to leave the reader with a sense of extraordinary gain would misrepresent Carver's sense of the human condition as encapsulated in a comment he made about "almost all the characters in my stories": "one single moment of revelation disrupts the pattern of their daily lives. It's a fleeting moment during which they don't want to compromise anymore. And afterwards they realize that nothing ever really changes" (*Conv*, 80).

5

In his introduction to *The Vintage Book of Contemporary American Short Stories* (1994), Tobias Wolff celebrated what he termed a renaissance in American short-story writing led by writers such as Carver "who bucked the fashion and got their stories straight from the well that had been posted stagnant by the preceding avant-garde." Wolff explained that while the dominant impulse in American short fiction had long been realistic, in the 1960s "we began to see a different kind of story here, resolutely nonrealistic, scholastic, selfconscious—*postmodern*—concerned with exploring its own fictional nature and indifferent if not hostile to the short story's traditional interests in character and dramatic development and social context." This was a serious matter, Wolff explained, because "The pleasure we take in cleverness and technical virtuosity soon exhausts itself in the absence of any recognizable human landscape. We need to feel ourselves acted upon by a story . . . the experience of something read can form us no less than the experience of something lived through" (xiii). For Wolff the great exemplar of this kind of short story is Chekhov. This is clear from the introduction to a volume of his stories Wolff edited in the late 1980s. There the Russian writer is described as "able to dissolve that safe distance between reader and story that convention maintains. The result is a sense of proximity and unpredictability." Even his early work, for example, contains "brief narratives of such density that they expand in the reader's memory when the act of reading is done." Wolff also insists that Chekhov "did not seek to reassure the reader by forcing his stories to uplifting conclusions, or by firing improbable insights and resolutions into the heads of his characters" (Chekhov 1988, xiv–xv).

This sounds as much like a description of the stories of Carver as it does those of Chekhov. Further similarities are intimated in Carver's last story, "Errand," which he wrote "to pay homage . . . [to] the writer who has meant so much to me for such a long time" (*Call*, 198). It is also Carver's most un-Carver-like story. Its first half, drawn entirely from the well of historical fact, recounts Chekhov's massive haemorrhage of the lungs during a dinner in 1896; Tolstoy's subsequent visit to him in hospital; his visit to a German spa in June 1904 with his wife, Olga; and what happened in his hotel room there on the night he died. Realizing that the author's death was imminent and there was nothing more to be done, the attending doctor was inspired to order a bottle of champagne. When handed a glass, Chekhov remarked that it had been a long time since he had drunk champagne, finished the glass, turned on his side, and a minute later died.

Having gotten this far into the story with the aid of a biography of Chekhov, Carver eventually realized that he now "needed to set my imagination free and simply invent within the confines of the story" (*Call*, 198). He invented a young waiter who brings the champagne and returns the next morning with a porcelain vase containing three long-stemmed yellow roses. He takes in the details of the room and immediately notices the cork from the champagne bottle on the floor near his foot, which he determines to bend over and pick up when he can do so unobtrusively. He waits while Chekhov's widow seems lost in thought. When she collects herself, Olga asks him to go out and bring back a mortician. She gives a detailed account of what will transpire during his errand, describing not only how he will behave but how the mortician will behave and even what he will say when he learns the name of the deceased. During her narration, the waiter remains preoccupied with the cork; when opportunity arises he leans over and closes his hand on it. With this action, the story ends.

On first reading, it might seem peculiar for Carver to pay homage to Chekhov in his most experimental story—the antithesis of the unselfconscious-seeming and unproblematic realism of the Russian writer. The explanation is found in a more nuanced sense of literary history in the late twentieth century than that provided by Tobias Wolff. As we have seen, Carver's career as a short-story writer begins intertextually with "The Cabin" and includes the metafictional "Put Yourself in My Shoes" and the self-reflexive "Intimacy." His canon thus provides evidence of what in 1972 Bernard Bergonzi called "the essentially problematic nature of fictional form in our time" (11). But unselfconscious mimesis is not a defining feature of realist representation, and self-reflexive and metafictional features in realist short stories do not preclude the creation of a human landscape or the communication of the experience of something lived through.

A number of what are defining features of the realist short story are implied in "Errand." One is the attention given to ordinary human experience —here that of the waiter who is on the periphery of the momentous event of a great writer's death, whose name has not survived, and who likely perished in the Great War. Another is commonplace objects—here the cork— that can become charged with implication. A third is the sense of tension, of something happening just below the surface—here the emotional turmoil of both Olga and the waiter. Finally there is the verisimilitude twice exemplified in "Errand": in Olga's narrative of what will happen to the waiter on his errand, which becomes so vivid it actually seems to be happening, as the shift to the present tense intimates; and more generally in the way that fictional events are seamlessly linked to historical events and kept on the same level of reality, thus suggesting the continuity and compatibility of the two realms. The same qualities also inform the work of my other subjects. Considered as short-story writers, one can say of all of them what Joyce said in praise of a story of Hemingway's—that they have "reduced the veil between literature and life . . . which is what every writer tries to do" (qtd. Power 1974, 107).

Afterword

In the preceding chapters, a critical model extrapolated from the comments of my subjects has been used for intentional readings of their short stories. Does this model have value for reading other realist short stories that feature verisimilitude plus a distinctive range of presentational features? I believe it does—in three important areas: understanding the importance of social context; understanding the status of meaning(s); and making qualitative discriminations. It is helpful to distinguish this model from the New Critical one that, to judge by numerous anthologies, is still the template for teaching short stories in the colleges and universities of North America. For Brooks and Warren in *Understanding Fiction,* "close analytical and interpretative reading of concrete examples" is the way that one can best be brought "to an appreciation of the more broadly human values implicit in fiction" (1959, xiii). This methodology involves essentialist presuppositions (instanced in their reading of Joyce's "Araby" which I critiqued in my third chapter) and leads to an underemphasis on the social and cultural context of stories. The same binary and the same underemphasis are found a generation later in Charles E. May's introduction to his influential edition of *The New Short Story Theories* (1994): "Short stories are . . . more apt to embody a timeless theme and are therefore less dependent on a social context than novels" (xxvi). And a decade later, May made essentially the same claim in different terms in his contribution to *The Art of Brevity: Excursions in Short Fiction Theory and Analysis* (2004).[1]

1. May writes, "If we assume that reality is what we experience every day, if we assume that reality is our well-controlled and comfortable self, then the short story is neither 'realistic' nor natural. If, however, we feel that beneath the everyday or immanent in the everyday there is some other reality that somehow evades us, if our view is a religious one in the most basic sense, that is, if we feel that something is lacking, if we have a sense of the liminal power of existence, then the short story

But in a realist short story, it is not a question of one or the other; it is rather that a distinctive feature of the form is its ability to combine both a social context and a theme that transcends that context. It is helpful to employ Helen Vendler's distinction between self and what she calls "soul." The former is a "socially specified human unit" shaped by locale, culture, ethnicity, nationality, sexuality, and so on. Soul is "the self when it is alone with itself, when its socially constructed characteristics . . . are felt to be in abeyance." For Vendler, "the normal mode of selfhood is the novel, [while] the normal home of 'soul' is the lyric" (1995, 5–7). While she is not concerned with short stories, Vendler's distinction is helpful in realizing that the realist short story often mediates between and fuses characteristics of both forms of being and that it is uniquely equipped to bring into sharp focus both the social self and the naked soul. Indeed a distinctive moment in the realist short story is the emergence of the latter from the mesh of constraining conditions in which the former exists.

Consider one of the best-known stories of each of my subjects. In Chekhov's "The Lady with the Little Dog," Gurov's resort-town affair with Anna (one in a repetitive series of casual adulterous relationships) begins to change into something more when they sit alone on a beach at dawn and look out at the sea. Its constancy and "utter indifference to the life and death of each of us" lead Gurov to reflect on higher matters—"the higher goals of being and our human dignity" (366–67). His soul, one might say, is touched, and his relation to Anna begins to change into an abiding love that will make his social existence seem increasingly false and secondary. Similarly, in Joyce's "The Dead," through the course of an evening's musical party, Gabriel Conroy moves from immersion in familial, marital, and cultural roles to a vision of last things: the snow falling on all of Ireland that he gazes at in the story's final paragraph is like the sea that Gurov contemplates—it brings a visionary moment of absorption of soul in a larger continuum of being. As in Hemingway's "The Snows of Kilimanjaro," the snow is also a symbol of death—of extinction of self. In present time in Hemingway's story, the self of the dying writer on the African plain is characterized by a brittle marriage and a failed career. Harry no longer thinks that there may be "some way he could work the fat off his soul the way a

---

is more 'realistic' than the novel can possibly be" (2004, 24). The distinction being made here is precisely the one between self and soul that I make below in arguing that the realist short story neither privileges nor excludes either term of May's binary opposition.

fighter went into the mountains to work and train in order to burn it out of his body" (60). It is only in a visionary moment of transcendence as he dies that his soul rises to the unbelievably white top of the mountain. In O'Connor's "A Good Man Is Hard to Find," the grandmother's self is vividly on display in the first half of the story in the social venues of family car and roadside restaurant. Under extraordinary pressure, it dissolves and is replaced by soul (with the supernatural connotations of the term operative) in the story's climactic moment as she looks into the eyes of her killer. And in Carver's celebrated "Cathedral," as we have seen, in the airy space of being of the title symbol the central character's self becomes free and undetermined—becomes soul.

It might seem from the critique of cultural-studies readings of *Dubliners* in my third chapter that in my view the realist story is little dependent on social context. It is rather that I disagreed with the view that Joyce's stories were merely the intended or unintended repository of cultural materials. In realist stories, a sense of social and cultural context is essential for the presentation of self. And in most cases—Hemingway's stories are an exception, as we have seen—it is also essential for the story's resonance. Another essential function of verisimilar context is pointed up by Robert Frost in a comment on the narrative poems of *North of Boston*, which are essentially realist short stories in blank verse. "Say what you will," he observes, "effects of actuality and intimacy are the greatest aim an artist can have. The sense of intimacy gives the thrill of sincerity. A story must always release a meaning more readily to those who read than life itself as it goes ever releases meaning. Meaning is a great consideration. But a story must never seem to be told primarily for meaning. Anything, an inspired irrelevancy even to make it sound as if told the way it is chiefly because it happened that way" (685).

It should go without saying that the meanings of short stories are important. As Frost insists, however, they are not the only essential elements and thus not the first, and not necessarily the preeminent, subject for critical consideration. But the New Critical mode of analysis privileged interpretation. Like the theoretically grounded discourses that were to "transform literary interpretation" by the mid-1980s (Hošek and Parker 1985, 7), this model emphasized the determination of meaning(s) and discouraged aesthetic and affective engagement with texts. With poetry, for example, "The whole process of explication [was] often a process of 'explicating' the implied cognitive content of metaphors or other figures in a poem" (Strier 1975–76, 176). I am by no means opposed to interpretative critical discourse per se and do not regard the aesthetic and the interpretative as mutually exclusive responses to a short story. But I am wary of the widespread assumption that "interpretation [is] the universal business of the humanities" (Nelson 1987, 47) and thus the principal business of literary criticism. I am particularly skeptical of what Robert D. Hume calls "*a priori* reading[s]"—that is, applications to a verbal artwork of systems of explanation, assumed by the critics using them to have privileged explanatory power, that are ungrounded in the work's distinctive properties (1999, 183)—like Christian exegetical readings of Chekhov's stories, some of the cultural-studies templates that have been applied to Joyce's stories, and some of the totalizing Christian interpretations of Flannery O'Connor's stories.

One is equally given pause by readings privileging indeterminacy. Allan Pasco has rightly complained that in his *The Modernist Short Story* Dominic Head raises the traits of conflicting voices and indeterminacy that he found in his subjects to "the status of generic characteristics for the short story as a whole" (Pasco 1993, 442). As I argued in my chapter on Joyce, Head's claims are suspect even in relation to the stories in *Dubliners* that are among his subjects. Another bold claim, made by Michael Trussler in his "Suspended Narratives: The Short Story and Temporality," is equally suspect. According to this critic, "Specifically rejecting the novel's inclination to deliberate and expound on reality, short stories . . . question the desire to confer significance upon an event by placing it in a larger, contextualizing pattern." Their brevity forces the reader to attend to the "metaphorical" dimensions of details in ways that increase "a text's indeterminacy." But "hermeneutical uncertainty does not lessen a story's apparent yearning for narrative closure." Indeed, "Short stories, in general, either implicitly or specifically project a hypothetical *continuation* of the narrative world created by the text, a postnarratorial existence"; but at the same time their brevity and intensity deny the existence of "a coherent contiguity that is extraneous to the text." (1996, 560–71). But of course the personified abstraction "short stories" is without agency and does none of these things. It is rather Trussler himself who has determined that the exclusive inter-art analogy for the short-story form is the novel and that interpretation in the hermeneutic sense is the kind of attention short stories demand. It is he who is the source of the uncertainty that he ascribes to the form, who apparently (but not really) yearns for narrative closure, and who both projects the continuation of the narrative world and denies its existence.

A better critical model for engaging with realist stories is one in which music or lyric is taken to be as relevant an inter-art analogy as the novel; in which there is no attempt to project the narrative beyond the stories' endings; and in which agency is attributed not to an abstraction but to the author, who in the case of Chekhov once observed that "My instinct tells me that at the end of . . . a story I must artfully concentrate for the reader an impression of the entire work" (Chekhov 1965, 17). An excellent example of such a concentrated impression is found at the end of "Rothschild's Fiddle," one of Chekhov's greatest stories. In nine pages, it offers in masterly combination everything a realist story can offer: artistic delight; the murmur of a containing society; affective power; cognitive import; and reflexive implication.

At the story's opening, the fiddle belongs to Yakov, an elderly village coffin-maker. Costive, hard-hearted, and quarrelsome, he views his past and present life as a series of losses, which he obsessively itemizes. "Never in good spirits, because he always had to suffer terrible losses," Yakov has a particular antipathy for the flutist Rothschild, "this cursed Jew [who] managed to play even the merriest things plaintively. For no apparent reason Yakov gradually began to be filled with hatred and contempt for the Jews, and especially for Rothschild" (254). As this quotation illustrates, the narrator of "Rothschild's Fiddle" adopts Yakov's point of view, language, and terms of reference. This obliges the reader "to perform an act of cautious 'translation,'" as Amos Oz puts it in an excellent discussion of the artistry of this story. His suggestion that the coffin-maker's detestation of Rothschild is "a clumsy, aggressive effort to suppress in himself" certain feelings is confirmed later in the story (1999, 51). The death of his wife of fifty years, and the recovery of the long-buried memory of the blond-headed baby who had died near the beginning of their married life, brings Yakov's obsession with the losses in his life to a crisis point: "why was the world ordered so strangely that life, which is given man only once, goes by without any benefit? . . . Everything in this world perished and would go on perishing!" In the story's climactic scene, Yakov sits with his fiddle on the step of his cottage: "Thinking about this perishing life of loss, he began to play, himself not knowing what, but it came out plaintive and moving, and tears flowed down his cheeks. And the harder he thought, the sadder the fiddle sang" (260–61).

That is to say, he is playing his fiddle in the same way that he had despised Rothschild for playing his flute. At this moment Rothschild arrives to deliver a message; then he pauses to listen as Yakov starts to play again with tears pouring from his eyes. As Rothschild listens, his frightened look gradually changing "to a mournful and suffering one, he rolled up his eyes as if experiencing some painful ecstasy and said: 'Weh-h-h!' . . . And tears flowed slowly down his cheeks." Yakov dies later that day, after having told the priest hearing his confession to give the fiddle to Rothschild. In the story's last paragraph, the narrator reports that a year later Rothschild had abandoned his flute for the fiddle and that "when he tries to repeat what Yakov had played as he sat on the step, what comes out is so dreary and mournful that his listeners weep. . . . And this new song is liked so much in town that merchants and officials constantly send for Rothschild and make him play it dozens of times" (251, 261–62).

One key to the power of this story is its economy of means—the "precise equilibrium" noted by Oz "between the ridiculous and the heart-breaking" and the way in which a limited, stunted person rises within a few pages "to the heights of tragic awareness" (1999, 50, 54). Another is the story's richness of conceptual implication. For one critic "Rothschild's Fid-dle" is "about the common Chekhov theme of loss and the lack of human communion" (May 1994, 212); for another, "the meaning is that we are all coffin-makers, all makers of categories, all refusing to fish in the great river of life and counting as losses what God has intended us to count as gain" (Frank O'Connor 1956, 256); and for Robert Louis Jackson, whose reading emphasizes the Russian Jewish cultural context, the story "links the parallel and tragic destinies of the Russian and the Jew," who are united in "an aesthetic humanism that lies beneath the disfigured surface of their lives" (Jackson 1987, 42, 38).

But the most conspicuous component of Chekhov's story is its unsettling affective impact, to which the story's reflexive level of implication calls attention. "Rothschild's Fiddle" exemplifies the same power that Roths-child's playing of the fiddle has on the townspeople who function within the story as the reader's surrogate. Their asking to hear Rothschild's new song over and over again suggests an unappeasable sense of loss and an unanswerable quandary as to why. "Everything inside me churns when I read 'Rothschild's Fiddle,'" Shostakovich remarked: "Who's right? Who's wrong? Who made life nothing but steady losses? Everything churns within me" (1979, 225). For this story Carver's analogy of a glimpse invested with power will not suffice. The perfect image is found in a comment by Eliza-beth Bowen: "We have within us a capacity, a desire, to respond. One of the insufficiencies of routine existence is the triviality of the demands it makes on us. Largely unused remain our funds of pity, spontaneous love, unenvious admiration or selfless anger. Into these, a story may drop a depth-charge" (1958, 1).

A third advantage of my aesthetic model is its usefulness in making and articulating qualitative discriminations among stories. When I became interested in the short-story form, I determined to read widely in realist short fiction of the twentieth century. I found many good stories and some I considered very good or even excellent. But after months of reading I found only a large handful of stories that I would rank with the finest stories of my subjects—despite the frequency with which the commentators I turned to for guidance used the term *masterpiece*. I was led to compare the body of material I had read to Wordsworth's poetry as described by Walter Pater: "Few artists . . . work quite cleanly, casting off all débris, and leaving us only what the heat of their imagination has wholly fused and transformed . . . the heat of [Wordsworth's] genius . . . has crystallised a part, but only a part, of [his work]; and in that great mass of verse there is much which might well be forgotten. But scattered up and down it," one found the real thing, fully fused and transformed, that it was the task of the aesthetic critic to identify (1980, xxi–xxii).

Realist short stories are small objects, and there seem to be as many of them as there are pebbles on a beach. One has a better chance of finding the gems among them if one knows what he or she is looking for. One feature of a fully crystallized work is faultless execution: every writer of a short story makes hundreds of presentational decisions from the macro to the micro—for example, from the choice of narrator, focalizer, and stylistic register, to the selection of dramatis personae and detail, to the positioning of a phrase or a word within a sentence and whether a character's utterance is quoted or paraphrased. A short story in which every choice seems perfectly made and nothing seems extraneous will engage the attention of good readers more deeply and lastingly than a less finished work. This, I would say, more than any other single quality is what distinguishes the short stories of Joyce—but of course he wrote only fifteen. A second quality is the story's ability to engage the affective attention of readers—to make them feel that something of consequence is being narrated and to move them. The third element is cognitive import—the sense, in Nadine Gordimer's formulation, that the story offers "a discrete moment of truth . . . not *the* moment of truth, because the short story doesn't deal in cumulatives" (1994, 265), but something that makes a reflective impression on the reader. When all three qualities are present in exceptional degrees in a realist story, the result is a masterly work of literary art such as "Rothschild's Fiddle" and a number of the stories discussed in the preceding chapters.

Works Cited

Abbott, H. Porter. 2002. *The Cambridge introduction to narrative.* Cambridge: Cambridge University Press.

Aldridge, John W. 1992. *Talents and technicians: Literary chic and the new assembly-line fiction.* New York: Scribner's.

Arias-Misson, Alain. 1982. "Absent talkers." *Partisan Review* 49:625–28.

Asals, Frederick. 1982. *Flannery O'Connor: The imagination of extremity.* Athens: University of Georgia Press.

Axelrod, Willa Chamberlain. 1993. "Passage from Great Saturday to Easter Day in 'Holy night.'" In Jackson, *Reading Chekhov's text,* 96–102.

Babel, Isaac. 2002. *Collected stories.* Ed. Nathalie Babel. Trans. Peter Constantine. New York: Norton.

Bacon, Jon Lance. 1993. *Flannery O'Connor and cold war culture.* Cambridge: Cambridge University Press.

Baldeshwiler, Eileen. 1994. "The lyric short story: The sketch of a history." In May, *The new short story theories,* 231–41.

Barney, Rick, et al. 1981. "Analyzing 'Araby' as story and discourse: A summary of the Murge project." *James Joyce Quarterly* 18:237–54.

Barth, John. 1984. *The Friday book: Essays and other nonfiction.* New York: Putnam's.

Bartlett, Rosamund. 2004. Introd. to Chekhov, *About love and other stories.*

———. 2000. "Shostakovich and Chekhov." In *Shostakovich in context.* Oxford: Oxford University Press, 199–218.

Bates, H. E. 1941. *The modern short story.* London: Nelson.

Bazargan, Susan. 2004. "Epiphany as a sense of performance." In *A new and complex sensation: Essays on Joyce's "Dubliners,"* ed. Oona Frawley. Dublin: Lilliput, 44–54.

Beegel, Susan F. 1998. "Second growth: The ecology of loss in 'Fathers and sons.'" In *New essays on Hemingway's short fiction,* ed. Paul Smith. Cambridge: Cambridge University Press, 75–110.

Beja, Morris. 1983. "One good look at themselves: Epiphanies in *Dubliners.*" In *Work in progress: Joyce centenary essays,* ed. Richard F. Peterson et al. Carbondale: Southern Illinois University Press, 3–14.

Belsey, Catherine. 1992. *Critical practice*. London: Routledge.

Ben-Porat, Ziva. 1976. "The poetics of literary allusion." *PTL: A Journal for Descriptive Poetics and Theory of Literature* 1:105–28.

Benson, Jackson J., ed. 1990. *New critical approaches to the short stories of Ernest Hemingway*. Durham: Duke University Press.

Bergonzi, Bernard. 1972. *The situation of the novel*. Harmondsworth, UK: Penguin.

Bishop, Elizabeth. 1992. *The complete poems: 1927–1979*. New York: Farrar, Straus.

Bitsilli, Peter M. 1983. *Chekhov's art: A stylistic analysis*. Trans. Toby W. Clyman and Edwina Jannie Cruise. Ann Arbor: Ardis.

Bleikasten, André. 1985. "The heresy of Flannery O'Connor." In *Critical essays on Flannery O'Connor*, ed. Melvin J. Friedman and Beverly Lyon Clark. Boston: G. K. Hall, 138–58.

———. 1982. "Writing on the flesh: Tattoos and taboos in 'Parker's back.'" *Southern Literary Journal* 14:8–18.

Bowen, Elizabeth. 1958. "Rx for a story worth the telling." *New York Times Book Review* (31 August): 1, 13.

Brooks, Cleanth, and Robert Penn Warren, eds. 1959. *Understanding fiction*. 2nd ed. New York: Appleton-Century-Crofts.

Budgen, Frank. 1960. *James Joyce and the making of "Ulysses."* Bloomington: Indiana University Press.

Carver, Raymond. 1985. "The cabin." In *Fires: Essays, poems, stories*. London: Collins Harvill, 145–56.

———. 2001. *Call me if you need me: The uncollected fiction and other prose*. Ed. William H. Stull. New York: Vintage.

———. 1984. *Cathedral: Stories*. New York: Vintage.

———. 1963. "Pastoral." *Western Humanities Review* 17:33–42.

———. 1989. *Where I'm calling from: New and selected stories*. New York: Vintage.

Chekhov, Anton. 2004a. *About love and other stories*. Trans. Rosamund Bartlett. Oxford: World's Classics.

———. 2004b. *The complete short novels*. Trans. Richard Pevear and Larissa Volokhonsky. New York: Everyman's Library.

———. 1988. *A doctor's visit and other stories*. Ed. Tobias Wolff. New York: Bantam.

———. 1964. *Lady with lapdog and other stories*. Trans. David Margarshack. London: Penguin.

———. 1973. *Letters of Anton Chekhov*. Ed. Simon Karlinsky. Trans. Michael Henry Heim. New York: Harper.

———. 1965. *Letters on the short story, the drama and other literary topics*. Ed. Louis S. Friedland. London: Vision.

———. 1985. *The party and other stories*. Trans. Ronald Wilks. London: Penguin.

———. 1960. *Selected stories*. Trans. Ann Dunnigan. New York: New American Library.

————. 2000. *Stories*. Trans. Richard Pevear and Larissa Volokhonsky. New York: Bantam.

Cheng, Vincent J. 1995. *Joyce, race, and empire*. Cambridge: Cambridge University Press.

Chudakov, A. P. 1983. *Chekhov's poetics*. Trans. Edwina Jannie Cruise and Donald Dragt. Ann Arbor: Ardis.

Cixous, Hélène. 1972. *The exile of James Joyce*. Trans. Sally A. J. Purcell. New York: David Lewis.

Clark, Miriam Marty. 1993. "After epiphany: American stories in the postmodern age." *Style* 27:387–94.

Conrad, Joseph L. 1977. "Anton Chekhov's literary landscapes." In *Chekhov's art of writing: A collection of critical essays,* ed. Paul Debreczeny and Thomas Eekman. Columbus, Ohio: Slavica, 82–99.

Cornwell, Gareth. 2005. "Mediated desire and American disappointment in the stories of Raymond Carver." *Critique: Studies in Contemporary Fiction* 46:344–56.

Crews, Frederick. 1992. "The critics bear it away." In *The critics bear it away: American fiction and the academy.* New York: Random House, 143–67.

Debreczeny, Paul. 2002. Introd. to *The lady with the little dog and other stories,* by Anton Chekhov. Trans. Ronald Wilks. London: Penguin.

Derman, Avram B. 1989. "Structural features in Chekhov's poetics." In *Critical essays on Anton Chekhov,* ed. Thomas A. Eekman. Boston: G. K. Hall, 34–44.

Ehrenburg, Ilya. 1969. "A speech at a Moscow meeting." In Isaac Babel, *You must know everything: Stories 1915–1937,* ed. Nathalie Babel. Trans. Max Hayward. New York: Farrar, Straus, 229–37.

Ehrlich, Heyward. 1998. "'Araby' in context: The 'splendid bazaar,' Irish orientalism, and James Clarence Mangan." *James Joyce Quarterly* 35:309–31.

Ellmann, Richard. 1982. *James Joyce*. Rev. ed. New York: Oxford University Press.

Engelstein, Laura. 1992. *The keys to happiness: Sex and the search for modernity in fin-de-siècle Russia*. Ithaca: Cornell University Press.

Ferguson, Suzanne C. 1996. "Defining the short story: Impressionism and form." In *Essentials of the theory of fiction,* ed. Michael J. Hoffman and Patrick D. Murphy. 2nd ed. Durham: Duke University Press, 287–300.

Fitzgerald, Sally. 1981–82. "Assumption and experience: Flannery O'Connor's 'A temple of the Holy Ghost.'" *Cross Currents* 31:423–32.

Flora, Joseph M. 1982. *Hemingway's Nick Adams*. Baton Rouge: Louisiana State University Press.

Frost, Robert. 1995. *Collected poems, prose, and plays.* Ed. Richard Poirier and Mark Richardson. New York: Library of America.

Furst, Lilian R. 1995. *All is true: The claims and strategies of realist fiction*. Durham: Duke University Press.

Gentry, Marshall Bruce, and William L. Stull, eds. 1990. *Conversations with Raymond Carver*. Jackson: University Press of Mississippi.

Girson, Rochelle. 1962. "Asphalt is bitter soil." *Saturday Review* (13 October): 20.

Goodheart, Eugene. 1987. "Raymond Carver's *Cathedral*." In *Pieces of resistance.* Cambridge: Cambridge University Press, 162–66.

Gordimer, Nadine. 1994. "The flash of fireflies." In May, *The new short story theories,* 263–67.

Grebstein, Sheldon Norman. 1973. *Hemingway's craft.* Carbondale: Southern Illinois University Press.

Gretlund, Jan Nordby. 2004. "Architexture in short stories by Flannery O'Connor and Eudora Welty." In Winther, *The art of brevity,* 151–61.

Gutsche, George J. 1999. "Moral fiction: Tolstoy's *Death of Ivan Il'ich*." In *Tolstoy's "The death of Ivan Il'ich": A critical companion,* ed. Gary R. Jahn. Evanston: Northwestern University Press, 55–101.

Hallett, Cynthia J. 1996. "Minimalism and the short story." *Studies in Short Fiction* 33:487–95.

Hanson, Clare. 1985. *Short stories and short fictions 1880–1960.* London: Macmillan.

———. 1989. "'Things out of words': Towards a poetics of short fiction." In *Rereading the short story.* London: Macmillan, 22–33.

Hawthorn, Jeremy. 2001. *Studying the novel.* 4th ed. London: Arnold.

Head, Dominic. 1992. *The modernist short story: A study in theory and practice.* Cambridge; Cambridge University Press.

Hemingway, Ernest. 1990. "The art of the short story." In Benson, *New critical approaches,* 1–13.

———. 1932. *Death in the afternoon.* New York: Scribner's.

———. 1999. *Ernest Hemingway on writing.* Ed. Larry W. Phillips. New York: Touchstone.

———. 1964. *A moveable feast.* New York: Scribner's.

———. 1972. *The Nick Adams stories.* Preface by Philip Young. New York: Scribner's.

———. 1981. *Selected letters 1917–1961.* Ed. Carlos Baker. New York: Scribner's.

———. 1953. *The short stories of Ernest Hemingway.* New York: Scribner's.

Herring, Philip F. 1987. *Joyce's uncertainty principle.* Princeton: Princeton University Press.

Hopkins, Gerard Manley. 1990. *Poetical works.* Ed. Norman H. MacKenzie. Oxford: Clarendon.

Hošek, Chaviva, and Patricia Parker, eds. 1985. *Lyric poetry: Beyond new criticism.* Ithaca: Cornell University Press.

Howe, Irving. 1994. *A critic's notebook.* Ed. Nicholas Howe. New York: Harcourt Brace.

Hume, Robert D. 1999. *Reconstructing contexts: The aims and principles of archaeo-historicism.* Oxford: Clarendon.

Iftekharrudin, Farhat, et al. 2003. Preface to *Postmodern approaches to the short story.* Westport, Conn.: Praeger.

Jackson, Robert Louis. 1993. "Chekhov's 'The student.'" In Jackson, *Reading Chekhov's text,* 127–33.

————. 1987. "'If I forget thee, o Jerusalem': An essay on Chekhov's 'Rothschild's fiddle.'" In Senderovich and Sendich, *Anton Chekhov rediscovered.*

————, ed. 1993. *Reading Chekhov's text.* Evanston: Northwestern University Press.

Jahn, Gary R. 1991. "A note on miracle motifs in the later works of Lev Tolstoi." In *Tolstoy's short fiction,* ed. Michael R. Katz. New York: Norton, 481–87.

James, Henry. 1984. *Literary criticism.* Ed. Leon Edel. 2 vols. New York: Library of America.

Joyce, James. 2000. *Dubliners.* Ed. Jeri Johnson. Oxford: Oxford University Press.

————. 1992. *A portrait of the artist as a young man.* Ed. Seamus Deane. London: Penguin.

————. 1975. *Selected letters.* Ed. Richard Ellmann. New York: Viking.

————. 1963. *Stephen hero.* Ed. Theodore Spencer. Norfolk, Conn.: New Directions.

————. 1986. *Ulysses: The corrected text.* Ed. Hans Walter Gabler. New York: Random House.

Karrer, Wolfgang. 1997. "Gnomon and triangulation: The stories of childhood in *Dubliners.*" In *New perspectives on "Dubliners,"* ed. Mary Power and Ulrich Schneider. Amsterdam: Rodopi, 458–68.

Kataev, Vladimir. 2002. *If only we could know! An interpreation of Chekhov.* Trans. Harvey Pitcher. Chicago: Ivan R. Dee.

Kershner, R. Brandon, ed. 2003. *Cultural studies of James Joyce.* Amsterdam: Rodopi.

Kessler, Edward. 1986. *Flannery O'Connor and the language of apocalypse.* Princeton: Princeton University Press.

Lainsbury, G. P. 2004. *The Carver chronotype: Inside the life-world of Raymond Carver's fiction.* New York: Routledge.

Leitch, Thomas M. 1989. "The debunking rhythm of the American short story." In Lohafer and Clarey, *Short story theory at a crossroads,* 130–47.

Levin, Richard L. 1989. "The problem of 'context' in interpretation." In *Shakespeare and the dramatic tradition: Essays in honor of S. F. Johnson,* ed. W. R. Elton and William B. Long. Newark: University of Delaware Press, 88–106.

Lodge, David. 1977. *The modes of modern writing.* Ithaca: Cornell University Press.

Lohafer, Susan, and Jo Ellyn Clarey, eds. 1989. *Short story theory at a crossroads.* Baton Rouge: Louisiana State University Press.

Luscher, Robert M. 1989. "The short story sequence: An open book." In Lohafer, *Short story theory at a crossroads,* 148–70.

Machotka, Pavel. 1996. *Cézanne: Landscape into art.* New Haven: Yale University Press.

Mansfield, Katherine. 1930. *Novels and novelists.* Ed. J. Middleton Murry. London: Constable.

Maugham, W. Somerset. 1967. "The human element." In *Complete short stories.* 3 vols. London: Heinemann, 991–1024.

———. 1963. *Selected prefaces and introductions.* London: Heinemann.

May, Charles E. 1990. "Artifice and artificiality in the short story." *Short Story* 1:72–82.

———. 1994. "Chekhov and the modern short story." In May, *The new short story theories,* 199–217.

———. 1993. "Reality in the modern short story." *Style* 27:369–79.

———. 2004. "Why short stories are essential and why they are seldom read." In Winther, *The art of brevity,* 14–25.

———, ed. 1994. *The new short story theories.* Athens: Ohio University Press.

McLain, Richard L. 1979. "Semantics and style–with the example of quintessential Hemingway." *Language and Style* 12:63–78.

Mihailovic, Alexander. 1993. "Eschatology and entombment in 'Ionych.'" In Jackson, *Reading Chekhov's text,* 103–14.

Mirsky, D. S. 1949. *A history of Russian literature.* Ed. Francis J. Whitfield. London: Routledge.

Mosher, Harold F., Jr. 1993. "The narrated and its negatives: The nonnarrated and disnarrated in Joyce's *Dubliners.*" *Style* 27:407–27.

Mullin, Katherine. 2003. *James Joyce, sexuality and social purity.* Cambridge: Cambridge University Press.

Nabokov, Vladimir. 1981. *Lectures on Russian literature.* Ed. Fredson Bowers. New York: Harcourt Brace.

Nakjavani, Erik. 1995. "The fantasies of omnipotence and powerlessness: Commemoration in Hemingway's 'Fathers and sons.'" In *Hemingway: Up in Michigan perspectives,* ed. Frederic J. Svoboda and Joseph J. Waldmeir. East Lansing: Michigan State University Press, 91–101.

Nelson, Cary. 1987. "Against English: Theory and the limits of the discipline." In *Profession 87.* New York: MLA, 45–52.

Norris, Margot. 2003. *Suspicious readings of Joyce's "Dubliners."* Philadelphia: University of Pennsylvania Press.

Oates, Joyce Carol. 1998. "The action of mercy." *Kenyon Review* 20:157–60.

O'Connor, Flannery. 1988. *Collected works.* Ed. Sally Fitzgerald. New York: Library of America.

———. 1984. *The complete stories.* New York: Farrar, Straus.

———. 1979. *The habit of being: Letters.* Ed. Sally Fitzgerald. New York: Farrar, Straus.

———. 1969. *Mystery and manners: Occasional prose.* Ed. Sally and Robert Fitzgerald. New York: Farrar, Straus.

O'Connor, Frank. 1968. *The lonely voice: A study of the short story.* New York: Bantam.

———. 1956. *The mirror in the roadway.* New York: Knopf.

O'Faolain, Sean. 1964. *The short story.* New York: Devin-Adair.

O'Toole, L. M. 1971. "Structure and style in the short story: Chekhov's 'Student.'" *Slavic and East European Review* 49:45–67.

Ouspensky, Leonid, and Vladimir Lossky. 1952. *The meaning of icons.* Boston: Bolton Book and Art Shop.

Oz, Amos. 1999. "Huge losses." *The story begins: Essays on literature.* New York: Harcourt Brace, 48–55.

Pasco, Allan H. 1993. "The short story: The short of it." *Style* 27:442–51.

Pater, Walter. 1980. *The renaissance: Studies in art and poetry.* Ed. Donald L. Hill. Berkeley: University of California Press.

Perri, Carmela. 1978. "On alluding." *Poetics* 7:289–307.

Phelan, James. 1998. "'Now I lay me': Nick's strange monologue, Hemingway's powerful lyric, and the reader's disconcerting experience." In *New essays on Hemingway's short fiction,* ed. Paul Smith. Cambridge: Cambridge University Press, 47–72.

Plimpton, George. 1963. "Ernest Hemingway." In *Writers at work: The Paris Review interviews.* 2nd series. New York: Viking, 217–39.

Poggioli, Renato. 1957. "Storytelling in a double key." In *The phoenix and the spider: A book of essays about some Russian writers and their view of the self.* Cambridge, Mass.: Harvard University Press, 109–130.

Pound, Ezra. 1954. *Literary essays.* Ed. T. S. Eliot. Norfolk, Conn.: New Directions.

Power, Arthur. 1974. *Conversations with James Joyce.* Ed. Clive Hart. Chicago: University of Chicago Press.

Prince, Gerald. 1987. *A dictionary of narratology.* Lincoln: University of Nebraska Press.

Pritchett, V. S. 1981. Introd. to *The Oxford book of short stories.* New York: Oxford University Press.

———. 2006. "[Who are these people?]." In *Katherine Mansfield's selected stories,* ed. Vincent O'Sullivan. New York: Norton, 344–46.

Proust, Marcel. 1981. *Remembrance of things past.* Trans. C. K. Scott Moncrieff and Terence Kilmartin. 3 vols. London: Chatto and Windus.

Rajan, Tilottama. 1981. *Dark interpreter: The discourse of romanticism.* Ithaca: Cornell University Press.

Rayfield, Donald. 1999. *Understanding Chekhov: A critical study of Chekhov's prose and drama.* Madison: University of Wisconsin Press.

Riquelme, John Paul. 1983. *Teller and tale in Joyce's fiction: Oscillating perspectives.* Baltimore: Johns Hopkins University Press.

Rosen, Nathan. 1985. "A Reading of Cexov's 'The lady with the dog.'" *Russian Language Journal* 39:13–29.

Rosenthal, M. L. 1978. *Sailing into the unknown: Yeats, Pound, and Eliot.* New York: Oxford University Press.

Rossetti, Dante Gabriel. 1961. *Poems.* Ed. Oswald Doughty. London: Dent.

Rovit, Earl. 1963. *Ernest Hemingway.* New York: Twayne.

Rubin, Louis D., Jr. 1977. "Flannery O'Connor's company of southerners: Or 'The artificial nigger' read as fiction rather than theology." *Flannery O'Connor Bulletin* 6:47–71.

Schaub, Thomas Hill. 1991. *American fiction in the cold war.* Madison: University of Wisconsin Press.

Senderovich, Savely. 1987. "Towards Chekhov's deeper reaches." In Senderovich and Sendich, *Anton Chekhov rediscovered,* 1–8.

Senderovich and Munir Sendich, eds. 1987. *Anton Chekhov rediscovered: A collection of new studies with a comprehensive bibliography.* East Lansing, Mich.: Russian Language Journal.

Senn, Fritz. 1969. "An encounter." In *James Joyce's "Dubliners": Critical essays,* ed. Clive Hart. London: Faber and Faber, 26–38.

Shaw, Valerie. 1983. *The short story: A critical introduction.* London: Longman.

Sherbinin, Julie W. de. 1997a. "Chekhov and Christianity: The critical evolution." In *Chekhov then and now,* ed. J. Douglas Clayton. New York: Peter Lang, 285–99.

———. 1997b. *Chekhov and Russian religious culture: The poetics of the Marian paradigm.* Evanston: Northwestern University Press.

Shloss, Carol. 1980. *Flannery O'Connor's dark comedies: The limits of inference.* Baton Rouge: Louisiana State University Press.

Shostakovich, Dmitri. 1979. *Testimony: The memoirs of Dmitri Shostakovich.* Ed. Solomon Volkov. Trans. Antonina W. Bouis. New York: Harper and Row.

Smith, Virginia Llewellyn. 1973. *Anton Chekhov and the lady with the dog.* London: Oxford University Press.

Stephens, Martha. 1973. *The question of Flannery O'Connor.* Baton Rouge: Louisiana State University Press.

Stevens, Wallace. 1961. *Collected poems.* New York: Knopf.

Strier, Richard. 1975–76. "The poetics of surrender: An exposition and critique of new critical poetics." *Critical Inquiry* 2:175–89.

Svoboda, Frederic Joseph. 1983. *Hemingway and "The sun also rises": The crafting of a style.* Lawrence: University Press of Kansas.

Tanner, Tony. 1967. *The reign of wonder: Naivety and reality in American literature.* New York: Harper and Row.

Terkel, Studs. 1974. *Working.* New York: Pantheon.

Thurston, Luke. 2004. *James Joyce and the problem of psychoanalysis.* Cambridge: Cambridge University Press.

Trilling, Lionel. 1979. *Prefaces to the experience of literature.* New York: Harcourt Brace.

Trussler, Michael. 1996. "Suspended narratives: The short story and temporality." *Studies in Short Fiction* 33:557–77.

Vendler, Helen. 1995. *Soul says: On recent poetry.* Cambridge, Mass.: Harvard University Press.

Wasiolek, Edward. 1978. *Tolstoy's major fiction.* Chicago: University of Chicago Press.

Weinstein, Arnold. 1993. "Flannery O'Connor and the art of displacement." In *Nobody's home: Speech, self, and place in American fiction from Hawthorne to DeLillo.* New York: Oxford University Press, 108–28.

Whitman, Walt. 1982. *Complete poetry and collected prose.* Ed. Justin Kaplan. New York: Library of America.

Wilde, Alan. 1987. *Middle grounds: Studies in contemporary American fiction.* Philadephia: University of Pennsylvania Press.

Winther, Per, et al., eds. 2004. *The art of brevity: Excursions in short fiction theory and analysis.* Columbia: University of South Carolina Press.

Wolff, Tobias. 1988. Introd. to Chekhov, *A doctor's visit and other stories.*

———. 1994. Introd. to *The Vintage book of contemporary American short stories.* New York: Vintage.

Woolf, Virginia. 1966. *Collected essays.* 4 vols. London: Hogarth.

Wordsworth, William. 1940–49. *Poetical works.* Ed. E. de Selincourt and Helen Darbishire. 5 vols. Oxford: Clarendon Press.

———. 1979. *The prelude 1799, 1805, 1850.* Ed. Jonathan Wordsworth et al. New York: Norton.

Young, Philip. 1971. "'Big world out there': The Nick Adams stories." *Novel* 6:5–19.

Zapf, Hubert. 1990. "Reflection vs. daydream: Two types of the implied reader in Hemingway's fiction." In Benson, *New critical approaches,* 96–111.

Index

About the Author

Kerry McSweeney is the Molson Professor of English at McGill University in Montreal, where he teaches courses in nineteenth- and twentieth-century British and American literature. His previous books include *The Language of the Senses: Sensory Perceptual Dynamics in Wordsworth, Coleridge, Thoreau, Whitman, and Dickinson; Supreme Attachments: Studies in Victorian Love Poetry;* and *What's the Import? Nineteenth Century Poems and Contemporary Critical Practice.*